100 ways to Make Poverty History

E 144 02

John Madeley is a writer and broadcaster who has specialized in Third World development and environmental issues for over 20 years. He regularly contributes to newspapers including the *Observer*, and is the author of several books on trade justice. He is a Church of England Lay Minister.

100 ways to Make Poverty History

An action kit to change your world

John Madeley

Illustrated by Dave Walker

CANTERBURY
PRESS

Norwich

First published in 2005 by the Canterbury Press Norwich
(a publishing imprint of Hymns Ancient & Modern Limited,
a registered charity)
9–17 St Albans Place, London N1 0NX

www.scm-canterburypress.co.uk

British Library Cataloguing in Publication data

A catalogue record for this book is available
from the British Library

ISBN 1-85311-683-1/9781-85311-684-1

Typeset by Regent Typesetting, London
Printed and bound by
Bookmarque, Croydon, Surrey

CONTENTS

Introduction

Two. Raising awareness of the issues

...AND IT MEANS WE DON'T NEED ANOTHER 'SAVE THE ROOF' APPEAL

For Eleanor, James, Isobel and Aoife.
May they visit that museum of poverty.

INTRODUCTION

Count to three seconds. If those three seconds are typical, a child will have died of poverty. That's enough to make you mad, hopping mad. A child dying helplessly, such a waste of life, of God-given talent.

Fine, feel mad. But move on – and get involved. This book contains a hundred ways in which you can get involved in making poverty history. Some of them you may already be doing. If you are doing all hundred – congratulations! In which case you'll want to give loads of copies of this book to your friends.

It is divided into six sections. The first is about persuading those in authority to change policies which hurt the poor. Second, how to raise awareness of the issues. The third section is about increasing your own understanding of the issues, the next one about using power – your purchasing power. The fifth section concerns changing the way you live. And finally – some tailpiece but key challenges.

Some of these challenges, like prayer, tithing and holding services, may be seen as specifically relevant for Christians. But the great majority of the hundred ideas are relevant for people of all religions and none.

Some of the suggestions are directly related to the Make Poverty History campaign . This is a fantastic, unprecedented effort, supported by over 500 organizations, including all the main churches and development organizations. The campaign was special in that it gave a number of unique opportunities for us to influence decision-makers. Hopefully it will be a landmark. It will see poverty put firmly on the path to becoming history.

But most of the ideas are for ongoing action. For at the end of the campaign the task of making poverty history will continue. In 2000, governments at a special United Nations General Assembly Summit unanimously made a promise – to halve the proportion of people living in poverty by 2015. It's one of the so-called Millennium Development Goals.

At present around 800 million people live in poverty. So the aim is to reduce that to 400 million – and to do it over the period from 2000 to 2015. Think ahead another 15 years – to 2030. If poverty could be reduced by 400 million between 2000 and 2015, it could be wiped out by 2030.

If you're an 18-year-old reading this book, that means by your early 40s poverty could be history. That's worth aiming at. So in addition to the suggestions in this book, make yourself a secret ambition – that in 2030 you will set up a museum of poverty. The museum would tell the history of poverty. It would tell of how Christians in the early part of the twenty-first century joined forces with others to say that poverty had gone on long enough, had persuaded those in power to act and not just speak, raised awareness of the issues and made changes in the way they live to help the effort. That's a museum you'd like your children to see. That would be a museum to glorify God.

But before then, there's an awful lot of work to do. The Millennium Development Goal on poverty is behind schedule. It will require a mighty effort from all of us to get it back on track. So an appeal. Maybe you personally have not so far been deeply involved in the poverty issue. But would you now make it your thing? If all of us take this on board, then something powerful can happen, we can make a real contribution to seeing that millennium goal achieved.

The Make Poverty History campaign has attracted the support of organizations not normally involved directly in poverty issues – like, for example, the Wycliffe Bible Translators, Alpha, the Musicians Union, etc. That's great; let's do the same personally.

In World War One there was a recruiting poster – Your Country Needs You. The task of making poverty history needs you – not that nice couple who live next door, well it needs them too, but it needs YOU. Thanks for buying this book. You're either some way down the track or at least on the starting block – and this is a race that's really worth winning.

My thanks to Christine Smith of SCM-Canterbury Press for encouraging me to write this book. And to Maranda St John Nicolle, co-ordinator of the Oxford-based Christian Concern for One World, who read the first draft and made some incisive and invaluable comments. Any mistakes are entirely mine.

John Madeley

One

Persuading those in authority to change policies which hurt the poor

1. Send a letter, card, e-mail to the Prime Minister to tell him how you feel about trade, aid and debt issues. Press in particular for trade justice, for fairer trade not free trade.

'The scandal of Africa isn't just that thousands of people died needlessly every day. The scandal is that they die when, with the right political will and effort, we can prevent their deaths.' Who says so? Tony Blair, on World Poverty Day.

So tell Mr Blair that you want poverty to be made history, in Africa, everywhere. And that action, not just talk, is needed for that. Stress how urgent this is, that you expect him to use his influence with other world leaders.

Ask him especially to stop pushing free trade on the poor. Tell him that the poor want justice in trade, not free trade. Tell him that trade liberalization has been disastrous for millions, that evidence is mounting that it does not over-come poverty.

Ask him to examine every government policy in the light of its impact on the poor.

You will be in good company. In the first four months of 2005 more than a quarter of a million people sent a mes-sage to Tony Blair and asked him to take advantage of the opportunity to beat poverty.

It would be electoral madness for the Prime Minister not to listen. So add your voice. Go to www.makepovertyhistory.org and click on Email Tony Blair. There's a letter to e-mail.

You can also e-mail the Prime Minister through www.number10.gov.uk.

Keep on reminding Mr Blair about the importance of the issues.

To post a letter or card, the address is: The Prime Minister, Rt Hon. Tony Blair MP, 10 Downing Street, London SW1A 2AA.

2. Tell the government you will serve it with an international ASBO unless it changes its anti-social behaviour and stops bullying poor countries.

Tanzania, one of the poorest countries, was threatened with aid cuts when it opposed the European Union at the World Trade Organization.

The EU will only make cuts in its agricultural subsidies if poor countries give European companies access to their financial and communications markets and cut industrial tariffs.

After being forced to slash tariffs by the International Monetary Fund and World Bank, (both effectively controlled by rich countries), the Zambian textile industry could not compete with cheap imports from industrialized countries. The sector has now all but vanished – 34,000 jobs have shrunk to 4,000.

This is bullying. Worse – it amounts to vandalism of developing country economies, to the lives of the poor. It has no place in a civilized world. People in Britain have had anti-social behaviour orders (ASBOs) served on them for less.

In April 2005, the World Development Movement, Friends of the Earth and War on Want served the leaders of Britain's three main political parties with an international ASBO. (See press release: www.wdm.org.uk/news/presrel/current/asbo.htm)

According to the UK Home Office the purpose of ASBOs is to 'target activities which disrupt the lives of individuals, families or communities.' But this is what rich countries are doing – disrupting lives. Tell the government, the WTO and the EU that you will slap an international ASBO on them unless they stop behaving like the neighbours from hell. To attract press attention, consider making a giant 'ASBO' and dressing people up as government, WTO, EU, etc.

3. Write to the Chancellor of the Exchequer to urge him to take urgent action to cancel 100 per cent of the unpayable debts of the poorest countries.

In May 1998, 70,000 people linked arms around Birmingham at the annual meeting of the world's eight most powerful leaders to demand DROP THE DEBT. The linked arms were a symbol of the chains of debt slavery. In 1999, at their meeting in Cologne, G8 leaders promised to cancel $100 billion of Third World debt.

Have they kept their promise? By May 2005, only $48 billion of debt had been cancelled and some western governments had raided their aid budgets to fund the relief. In June 2005 another $40 billion was agreed, making $88 billion in all, still less than the 1999 promise.

Debts of poor countries now total $523 billion. Every day the world's most impoverished countries are forced to pay over £30 million to the rich world in debt repayments. This is a scandal. The money could have been used for anti-poverty projects such as providing more classrooms, clean water, improved health facilities, etc.

Rich countries should stop making debt relief conditional on poor countries privatizing and liberalizing their economies. That's an infringement of the right of elected governments to decide policies. So write to the Chancellor to urge him to end this scandal and cancel 100 per cent of debts – and do it quickly.

World Debt Day is held each year on 16 May. Use it to publicize the debt scandal.

Chancellor of the Exchequer, HM Treasury, 1 Horse Guards Parade, London sw1a 2hq.

Jubilee Debt Campaign, 28 Charles Street, London n1 6ht; tel: 020 7324 4722; web: www.jubileedebtcampaign.org.uk

4. Urge the government to use its presidency of the European Union to stop imposing free-market Economic Partnership Agreements on Africa.

Partnership is a fine thing, or at least it can be. Putting it down on paper and making an agreement about it, may be useful. But so called 'partnerships' between rich and poor countries have often done nothing for the poor.

The EU and 46 countries in Africa, the Caribbean and the Pacific (ACP) signed an agreement on trade and aid in 1975 called the Lomé Convention. It ran for 25 years but did little to reduce poverty in most of the ACP countries.

Another agreement was signed between the EU and the ACP in 2000 – the Cotonou Agreement. By then the number of ACP countries had grown to 78. But this is in danger of being even less useful than Lomé. It could reinforce rather than reduce poverty.

For under the Cotonou Agreement, the EU wants to impose free-trade Economic Partnership Agreements (EPAs) on its poorer neighbours. It wants the ACP countries to eliminate all barriers on 90 per cent of trade between the two blocs. This would mean that nearly all the tariffs and other barriers on European agricultural and industrial goods to ACP countries would be scrapped. It's survival of the fittest – the richest. EU countries have the funds to exploit the new market opportunities. They stand to benefit far more than the poorer countries. So who is helping whom?

The EPAs could be a disaster for poor countries. Holding the presidency of the EU, the UK government should use its influence to stop EPAs worsening poverty. Press the government to offer ACP countries an alternative form of partnership.

The Traidcraft website has a good summary of EPAs (www.traidcraft.co.uk).

5. Press government ministers to end the West's farm subsidies. These have caused large surpluses to be produced which have been dumped in developing countries and have bankrupted farmers.

Every year the EU, through its Common Agricultural Policy, and the United States and other western country governments, hand their farmers over $100 billion in subsidies. And they spend another $200 billion in indirect supports – including, for example, funds for research and development.

That sum of money is higher than the combined national incomes of sub-Saharan African countries. It encourages farmers in western countries to produce more than is needed. There's a surplus, some of which is then dumped – sold below the cost of production – in developing countries. This dumped food has driven millions of poor farmers into bankruptcy. Their produce could not compete on local markets with the imported food.

In 2003 the EU announced changes in its Common Agricultural Policy, but the changes will not end dumping. While the West uses subsidies, it preaches free trade at the poor. Little wonder that Chancellor

of the Exchequer, Gordon Brown, has said that countries should 'end the hypocrisy of developed country protectionism' and do more 'to urgently tackle the scandal and waste of the Common Agricultural Policy'.

Remind the Chancellor that it's action not words that will remove this burden from the poor (address as above).

6. Urge the government to meet the United Nations aid target and give 0.7 per cent of our national income in aid, and to ensure that it benefits the poor.

Aid of the right kind is needed to help make poverty history. The rich sharing some of their wealth is not only right but a duty. This was recognized in 1970 when the United Nations General Assembly adopted a target – rich countries should aim to provide at least 0.7 per cent of their national income in aid.

Yet 35 years later, only five western countries are doing that. Britain gave 0.36 per cent of its national income in aid in 2004.

The UK government is committed to reaching the UN target by 2013. That is too far away. It needs to reach the target by the end of the current parliament, 2009 or 2010.

Gordon Brown has proposed to increase aid with an International Finance Facility that would borrow money on the international capital markets, on the basis of aid already committed. Some of the Make Poverty History groups have reservations, fearing it could affect future aid levels. Neither is more aid alone enough. It needs to be aid that really benefits the poor.

Aid should focus on needs. More is needed for education and healthcare, to tackle and deal with the causes of HIV/AIDS, for example. Aid should support poor countries and communities' own plans and paths out of poverty. Rich countries should stop making their aid conditional on recipients privatizing their economies – which has never been proven to reduce poverty. The British government has announced that it will stop doing this. But again it's action that is needed.

Write to the Chancellor of the Exchequer, and to Hilary Benn, International Development Secretary, DFID, 1 Palace Street, London SW1E 5HE.

7. Remind the government that it promised in 2000 to halve the number of people living in poverty by 2005, and that this is the one promise above all you want it to keep.

Promises, promises. At election times, we get so many of them, and perhaps boggle as to where the money is coming from. In our minds, we might downsize such promises. But there is one promise above all we expect the government to keep.

In 2000, at a millennium summit of the United Nations General Assembly, 189 governments committed themselves to Millennium Development Goals – eight in all – covering poverty, education, health, gender equality and the environment. All are to be met by 2015.

Goal number one is to 'eradicate extreme poverty and hunger', specifically to 'reduce by half the proportion of people living on less than a dollar a day, and reduce by half the proportion of people who suffer from hunger'. In 2005 we're a third of the way to 2015, and the poverty goal is behind schedule. It will not be met unless progress is speeded up.

In September 2005 the UN General Assembly meets to assess progress. Governments need to take the lack of progress seriously. Millions more will die if these goals are not met. They are too important to lose. They are but a step to making poverty history. But they're an important step.

8. Write to the heads of the World Bank and the International Monetary Fund (IMF) and ask them to look again at their policies as they affect the poor.

The World Bank funds projects in developing countries while its sister organization, the IMF, assists with balance of payments problems. In practice, the World Bank is a fund and the IMF is a bank.

Confused? World Bank policies are confused. The mast on the World Bank's website reads: 'Working for a World Free of Poverty'. Yet many World Bank policies appear to reinforce poverty. In the early 1990s, together with the IMF, the Bank devised Structural Adjustment Programmes (SAPs). Developing countries had to implement these if they wanted aid, debt relief and investment.

SAPs are supposed to lead to economic recovery, long-term growth and stability. Instead SAPs have led to economic stagnation, mass unemployment and increased poverty. In most countries they have not led to the higher economic growth they were supposed to be all about.

In the mid-1990s the World Bank gave funds to Vietnam to produce more coffee. The result was a flood of coffee onto the world market and low prices which drove coffee farmers in every developing country into poverty. The free play of market forces, that the Bank and the Fund embrace, is not consistent with a world free of poverty.

Write to the heads of the Bank and Fund and ask them to look at their projects through the eyes of the poor.

Paul Wolfowitz, President, The World Bank, 1818 H Street NW, Washington DC 20433, USA.
Rodrigo de Rato, Managing Director, IMF, 19th Street NW, Washington DC 20431, USA.
The Bretton Woods Project monitors the Bank and the IMF (www.brettonwoodsproject.org).

9. Press the World Trade Organization to recognize the negative effects of trade liberalization on the poor.

Set up in 1995, the WTO is one of the newer international organizations. And also one of the most controversial.

The WTO made world headlines in 1999 when street protests marked its ministerial meeting in the US city of Seattle. People took to the streets in their tens of thousands to protest that the meeting had been called to launch a new round of trade liberalization that would reinforce poverty.

The meeting failed as surely as the WTO fails to recognize that liberalization has been a disaster for millions of poor people. The WTO gives the impression that it is barely aware of the many studies – from both official and NGO sources – which show the damaging impact of trade liberalization, or free trade, on the poor, particularly in vital areas like food security.

The poor would benefit from more trade, claims the WTO. But it would do well to estimate how much of the claimed benefit from additional trade from liberalization will accrue to the traders, such as transnational corporations, and how much to the poor.

The WTO needs to shows more awareness that it is companies not the poor who trade on world markets. The organization has a new director-general, Mr Pascal Lamy. Write to Mr Lamy, point to the evidence and ask him to reassess the WTO's direction. WTO, Centre William Rappard, Rue de Lausanne 154, CH-1211 Geneva 21, Switzerland.

For evidence:

Trade and hunger – an overview of case studies on the impact of trade liberalization on food security, Forum Syd, www.forumsyd.se/globala.htm

The impact of trade liberalization on food security in the South, Literature Review, CIDSE, www.cidse.org.

10. Urge the government to end its support for the privatization of water supplies in developing countries.

When water was privatized in Puerto Rico, poor communities went without water, while US military bases and tourist resorts enjoyed an unlimited supply. When water was privatized in Bolivia, there were riots in the streets. Several people died.

Many people do not have access to clean water – around 1.3 billion according to the UN. It takes genius to devise a scheme that would increase, not decrease, the number of people without water. Yet this is what the WTO's General Agreement on Trade in Services (GATS) does. The aim of the GATS is to remove any restrictions and regulations in services, such as water supply, that are considered 'barriers to trade'.

The UK was the first country to privatize water (in 1989). When private companies take over water supplies they expect

payment. This may be fine in rich countries, but millions of the poor have no money. They are outside the money economy.

Defeating poverty and privatizing water are opposites. A system governed by people's ability to pay will not bring desperately needed services to people who live in poverty.

Yet EU governments support the privatization of water supplies. But this is free trade ideology gone mad. Water should be a public good, not a private money-spinner. Write and urge the government to stop this water nonsense.

The World Development Movement is campaigning on the inequities of the GATS. On water privatization, see its report *Dirty Water* (www.wdm.org.uk).

11. Press for the Tobin Tax on international currency speculation.

Imagine a pile of £50 notes stretching from the earth to the moon. That's about the size of the world money market each year. Some USD 1,000 billion of currency is bought and sold each day. A small amount of this – some 5 per cent – is for trade and other real economic transactions. But 95 per cent is for pure speculation. Companies and individuals buy and sell dollars, euros, pounds, yen, etc. in the hope of befitting from tiny movements in currency values. Whether currencies move up or down, speculators have learned how to make a profit.

This speculation is unregulated and untaxed. It plays havoc with national budgets and economic planning. It has been linked to the 1997–98 currency crisis in Southeast Asia, the failure of the European exchange-rate mechanism in 1992, and lay behind the 'Black Wednesday' devaluations and loss of national revenue in September that year.

In 1978 James Tobin, a Nobel prize-winning economist, proposed that a small tax (less than 0.5 per cent) be levied on foreign exchange transactions to deter currency speculation.

The tax would not only check speculation it would also yield a considerable sum. Even at a rate of 0.2 per cent, the tax could yield USD 150 billion annually – around twice as much as annual development aid from rich to poor countries.

The Tobin tax could add stability to economies and generate substantial additional resources to defeat poverty. It is hard to think of a more painless way of achieving both.

Urge the Chancellor of the Exchequer to promote the Tobin Tax and secure its international acceptance.

War on Want campaigns on the Tobin Tax (www.waronwant. org/?lid=2).

12. With climate change likely to worsen poverty, call for stricter limits on emissions of the gases that cause global warming.

In September 2004 Tony Blair made a speech in which he described climate change as 'the world's greatest environmental challenge, and so far reaching . . . it alters radically human existence'*.

A report *Up in Smoke* says that global warming threatens to reverse human progress 'and make the international targets on halving global poverty by 2015 unattainable' (www.christian aid.org.uk/indepth/410smoke/index.htm).

Climate change is caused by increased levels of carbon dioxide and other polluting greenhouse gases in the atmosphere. The government has promised to cut emissions of carbon dioxide by 20 per cent from 1990 levels by 2010, and by 60 per cent by 2050.

It is well behind target. Between 1990 and 2003, greenhouse gas emissions fell by 8.1 per cent, according to the Office of National Statistics, the fall coming as a result of the one-off closure of coal mines.** Greenhouse gas emissions from UK air industry doubled in these 13 years. Existing government policies will not do. Urge the government to make the fight against climate change a priority.

Climate change affects us all, but hits hardest at the poor. The government's actions must match its words. The Friends of the Earth campaign, The Big Ask, calls for climate change law. This would force the government to take responsibility for the UK's contribution to global warming by reducing carbon dioxide emissions by 3 per cent every year (www.foe.co.uk). See Tearfund:
www.tearfund.org/Campaigning/Issues/Climate+change.htm.

Also Operation NOAH:
www.christian-ecology.org.uk/noah/index.htm.

*14 September 2004:
www.number-10.gov.uk/output/page6333.asp

**19 May 2005: www.statistics.gov.uk/pdfdir/enacco505.pdf

13. Call for an early end to government subsidies for the aviation industry, and for an end to airport expansion.

Emissions of gases at high altitude have a greater impact on the atmosphere than ground-level emissions. The aviation sector is now set to become the largest cause of greenhouse gas emissions.

The British government subsidizes the UK aviation industry with more money than it gives to the world's poor in aid. The industry benefits from £9.2 billion in subsidies (as against £4.3 billion in aid), say Friends of the Earth. The benefit comes through a variety of tax breaks – the main one being no tax or VAT is payable on aviation fuel.

By 2010 the increase in emissions from aviation would play

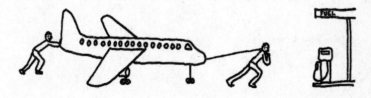

havoc with the commitments the government has under the Kyoto Protocol, says the House of Commons Environment Audit Committee: 'The UK's 60 per cent carbon emissions reduction target . . . will become meaningless and unachievable' (www.parliament.uk).

If the government is serious about tackling global warming, it should end aviation subsidies. And drop plans to build new airports and runways.

14. Press for taxes on aviation fuel.

They are called cheap flights and so they are by some reckoning. But the flights we take to a sunny place for £9.99 or whatever are not cheap at all. The bill is being paid by someone.

In practice the bill is being paid by us all, by our environment. And the knock-on effect is felt by the poor.

Cheap flights are possible because there are no taxes on the fuel that aircraft guzzle. Tax is paid on fuel for vehicles. Why not for aircraft? The government has set its face against taxes on aviation fuel. Economic growth would be affected, it claims. Furthermore, it could only be done by international agreement.

But economic growth could be affected far more seriously in the future unless greenhouse gas emissions from aircraft are checked. The government could introduce a tax on fuel for domestic flights. It does not need international agreement for this. Neither is there anything to stop the government increasing air passenger duty.

An alternative to a fuel tax is an emissions charge on aircraft. What is important is that the government does something that is effective.

15. Press the World Intellectual Property Organization to take development on board.

Intellectual Property Rights may seem to have scant connection with poverty. Until the 1980s you would have been hard pressed to find one. Intellectual Property Rights (IPRs) then covered just industrial, patents, trademarks, copyrights, etc. These rights protect the right of the holder for a given period.

But in the 1980s US-based companies began to apply for and were granted US patents on plants and seeds. They are controversial – what right have we to patent parts of God's creation? They also have considerable implications for the poor.

A US-based company has taken out patents on basmati rice, for example, which has been grown for centuries in Asia. Transnational corporations have applied for over 50 patents on crops and species that grow in India. Farmers are concerned that these patents could mean they have to pay corporations for the right for plant crops they use.

Crops apart, drugs companies have patented medicines that treat HIV/AIDS. But their cost is often too high for developing countries to get them in the quantities they need.

In 1995 IPRs were internationalized when the WTO came into being. The WTO's Trade-Related Intellectual Property Rights (TRIPS) agreement. This requires member countries of the WTO to adopt standards for the protection of intellectual property – in other words, to protect the patent-holder.

The World Intellectual Property Organization, a Geneva-based UN agency, has the task of 'promoting the use and protection of works of the human spirit'. Press WIPO to take a more development approach and establish an intellectual property system that safeguards the rights of the poor (www.wipo.int).

Third World Network campaigns on this issue (www.twnside.org.sg).

16. Insist that the international economic system gives people the right to food as laid down in international law.

Everyone has the right to adequate food, the right to be free from hunger. Article 25 of the United Nations Universal Declaration of Human Rights spells it out: 'everyone has the right to a standard of living adequate for the health and well-being of himself and his family, including food, clothing, health and medical care . . .'

Yet around 800 million are denied this right. Without adequate food, they lack the nourishment to develop their full potential. Civil and political rights may mean little for the person who must devote her or his resources to finding enough food to stay alive.

Some 21 countries have enshrined food rights explicitly in their national constitution. And to be able to enjoy the right to food, people also need access to healthcare and education. Ensuring the right to food also involves factors such as opportunities for earning income, access to land, water and financial assets, and efficient and fair market systems.

Nobel laureate Amartya Sen gave the world the theory of 'entitlements' – that famines don't happen when people have an entitlement to food. But governments have failed to develop a global economic system that would give the poor 'entitlements' to food – or to consider the changes needed to develop that kind of system. Remind the government of its obligation to ensure that everyone has enough food.

A paper: 'Should we provide a guarantee that no child will be brain-damaged by malnutrition in Africa if money can prevent it?' can be viewed on www.odi.org.uk.

17. Write to foreign governments. Let them know that you care about what they do, and hold them to the same standards of human decency as you hold your own government.

Governments throughout the world are likely to know about the Make Poverty History campaign. The campaign is part of a wider international effort, the Global Call to Action Against Poverty. Trade justice, debt relief and more and better aid will deliver more resources to developing countries for the fight against poverty.

Not all governments use resources wisely, however. According to Transparency International's index '106 out of 146 countries score less than 5 against a clean score of 10' – where 10 is no corruption and 0 is the opposite.

Sixty countries score less than 3 out of 10, indicating rampant corruption. Corruption is perceived to be most acute in countries such as Bangladesh, Haiti, Nigeria, Chad and Burma, all of which have a score of less than 2.

Corruption, poor governance, robs the poor. But poverty still exists in countries where corruption is relatively light – in, for example, Chile which scores 7.4 on the index. (The UK scores 8.6, the US 7.5.)

The international community 'has a role to play in maintaining high standards of governance', says the Africa Commission report. 'If it does so in its own activities – and demands it in the activities of private sector agents, like the multinational companies active in developing countries – then it will be better positioned to encourage similar high standards.'

Encouraging high standards is vital for governments in both developing and developed countries.

Africa Commission, www.commissionforafrica.org
Transparency International, www.transparency.org

18. Buy a single share in a transnational corporation that is involved in developing countries.

Of the world's 100 largest economies 49 are countries, 51 are transnational corporations (TNCs). General Motors is bigger than Denmark and over three times the size of New Zealand. The top 200 corporations have combined sales larger than the combined economies of all countries, except the largest ten.

Size gives corporations power to influence national and international decisions, including trade rules. Two-thirds of world trade is between the corporations. In the twenty-first century it is companies that trade not countries. And there's the problem – we elect governments, we do not elect corporations. TNCs are public companies that are owned by shareholders.

But shareholders have at least a degree of power in the way their company is run. So buy a single share in a company that is active in developing countries and monitor its activities.

People concerned about TNC activity and power have been doing this at least since the 1970s. The World Development Movement then encouraged its members to buy a single share in the tea company Brooke Bond and in the tobacco company BAT.

Today you might be interested in buying a share in an oil corporation that is accused of stripping Africa of its wealth. As a shareholder you will receive all the company reports and you see what it's doing. Research the company carefully. Make yourself a specialist in its activities. E-mail, write to the chief executive to ask questions.

Single shares can be purchased from a bank or stockbroker. Be warned that the cost of buying just one share may be higher than the value of the share, but it's a one-off cost. Some companies allow you to buy a share direct from them. It's worth calling them to check.

19. Attend the annual meeting of companies in which you hold a share, raise questions from the floor and table a resolution with other shareholders.

With a single share you are entitled to attend the annual meetings of your company. Single shareholders have been doing this for years. There are two things you can do:

1 Ask a question from the floor. You may be concerned about how the company's activities are affecting a poor community in a certain country. Not only will the board of directors hear of your concern but so also will the assembled shareholders – and there could be several hundred of them. You may be given a bland reply – but your concern could influence policy.
2 Table a resolution urging the company to put right an injustice. As a shareholder you have every right to do this. (You may be required to own a certain number of shares to put forward a resolution.)

Your resolution may be defeated – be prepared for it to be heavily defeated – but it could gain media publicity, highlight the injustice and change company policy.

For example, at the annual meeting of Shell in May 1997, 130 shareholders tabled a resolution that requested Shell to 'establish an independent review and audit procedure' for its environmental and human rights policies. It was supported not only by NGOs such as Amnesty International, but also by 18 pension funds.

Although the resolution was defeated, the company accepted the principle of external verification of the company's performance. Shareholder pressure paid off. So get together if you can with other shareholders. An NGO that campaigns on the issue might be helpful with this – Baby Milk Action on Nestlé, and other milk companies, for example (www.baby milkaction.org).

20. Support calls by Christian Aid and other agencies for international regulation of big business.

Never in human history has a comparatively small number of private corporations wielded so much power . . . the power of the TNCs needs to be brought under democratic control. (Master or Servant?, Christian Aid)

Corporations are powerful but unregulated at least at the international level. This is not right. Corporations cannot be trusted to regulate themselves.
The British government is promoting a deregulatory agenda, but there is an urgent need for more effective regulation of corporations as they affect developing countries.

Christian Aid propose that a Global Regulatory Authority (GRA) be set up. The GRA would:

• Draw up and establish a code of conduct for TNCs.
• Monitor compliance with the code.

- Have a citizens' support unit to help organizations bring cases in national courts.
- Conduct investigations into breaches.
- Have the power to make legally binding rulings against TNCs breaching the codes.
- Set minimum standards for the disclosure of information on TNC activities.
- Monitor market abuses, such as cartels and monopolies.
- Monitor direct foreign investment and advise on whether it would contribute to sustainable development.

Other agencies, including Friends of the Earth, have also made proposals that deserve support if TNCs are to be more accountable.

www.christian-aid.org.uk
www.foe.co.uk

21. Clean up your computer!

Take a closer look at your computer. Have you ever thought about how it was made? Or who by?

More than a third of electronic goods are made in poor countries. Evidence has been uncovered by Cafod that thousands of workers are exploited to make our hi-tech machines, especially in Thailand, Mexico and China.

The three computer giants, IBM, Dell and Hewlett-Packard, have been encouraged by campaigners to develop codes of conduct for working conditions. But the companies need to ensure that workers throughout their supply chains have the right to join a trade union. This is essential for real and lasting improvements in factory conditions.

Send an e-mail in your own words to IBM, Dell and Hewlett-Packard:

Mark Hurd, CEO HP
hp.globalcitizenship@hp.com

Michael Dell, CEO Dell
Sustainability_EMEA@dell.com

Sam Palmisano, CEO IBM
bm_crc_uk@vnet.ibm.com

If you go to the Cafod website – www.cafod.org.uk – and click on 'Clean up your computer', there is a prepared e-mail to send to all three.

22. Call for an end to the trade in armaments and the massive subsidies which the government hands to the armaments industry.

Armed conflicts are the leading cause of world hunger, says the UN Food and Agriculture Organization. But where do the arms come from? Mostly from the West, many from Britain. British companies sell arms all over the world, including to countries with poor human rights records, such as Indonesia, Saudi Arabia and Nigeria. The industry receives government subsidies amounting to over £800 million a year.

Many churches, including the Church of England, the Roman Catholic Church and the Society of Friends, have taken a strong stand on the morality of the arms trade. A Quaker statement brings out the link between armaments and poverty:

> We believe the arms trade to be morally wrong. It encourages governments to seek military solutions to political problems and adds to the suffering in any resulting conflict . . . the resources spent to manufacture and to buy them are diverted forever from essential human needs such as food and health care . . . the global trade in arms makes the world less, not more secure.

It also makes the world more poor. The Campaign Against Arms Trade (CAAT) works for the reduction and ultimate abolition of the international arms trade.

The CAAT Christian Network was formed in 1994 by a number of Christian supporters of CAAT. It works with other Christian organizations to raise awareness of arms trading within churches and provides resources for Christians wishing to study the issues. It holds an annual Day of Prayer in June (www.caat.org.uk).

Another campaign, The Control Arms campaign, consists of organizations in over 70 countries. It is urging governments to adopt an Arms Trade Treaty (www.controlarms.org). See also the SPEAK campaign (www.speak.org.uk/node/50).

23. Get your name onto the mailing lists of Make Poverty History, Christian Aid, Cafod, etc. and respond to requests to write to people in authority on specific issues.

Poverty and development issues are fast moving. Things happen all the time. Some reach the press, many don't. You cannot watch everything.

But the aid and development agencies monitor very carefully what is going on, and when the need arises, they will ask supporters to write to people in government, the WTO, the World Bank, etc. about a pressing issue.

After the last UK General Election, for example, Comic Relief asked people on its e-mail list to contact Tony Blair to remind him of what he said about the scandal of people dying from poverty. Tens of thousands responded within days.

You may be asked to come to a rally or to urge your MP to sign an Early Day Motion on a development issue. So get your name onto the sites of as many as you can – and when the need arises, respond quickly.

Here are some of the main ones:

Make Poverty History, a network of over 500 organizations.
www.makepovertyhistory.org

Christian Aid, the church's aid agency in the UK.
www.christian-aid.org.uk
Cafod, Catholic Agency for Overseas Development
www.cafod.org.uk

Tearfund, works with Christian agencies and churches worldwide to tackle poverty
www.tearfund.org

Comic Relief, launched in 1985 in response to the African famine
www.comicrelief.com

SPEAK, a prayer and campaigns network for students and young people
www.speak.org.uk

24. At election time, vote for the party with the best policies on development issues.

Elections offer a good opportunity for voters to demonstrate their concern for the poor to election candidates, and to push them on key issues.

At election time, the political parties treat you as a specially valued person. Well they would do, they need your vote! Tell the candidates that your vote will go the party with the best policies for making poverty history.

For the 2005 election, the World Development Movement published a guide to party policies 'Where the parties stand on justice for the world's poor', awarding the parties marks out of 10. This can be viewed on: www.wdm.org.uk/campaigns/election/index.htm

Read the manifestos and write to the candidates and ask them where they stand personally on the issues. Then go to their meetings and ask them questions. In most constituencies a number of all-party meetings take place. Often the churches organize a meeting to look especially at moral issues. If there isn't one near you, organize one!

In between elections, there's work to do, as prospective candidates are often chosen two or three years beforehand. Ask to meet them and find out where they stand.

25. Keep your MP and your MEP informed about your views and activities.

'If I get five letters a week on one subject, I take notice. If I get 20, I get worried.'

This is how one Member of Parliament viewed her mailbag. So write to your MP often. Send copies of letters you send to the Prime Minister and the Chancellor to your MP, and ask them if they would also take up the matter.

Make sure your friends do the same – and get your MP

worried. Some churches organize letter-writing sessions on key issues. The letters to your MP serve as a barometer of public feeling. They are ignored at the MP's risk. It can be worth asking your MP to put a question to the relevant government minister or department.

You may know the name of your MP – but you cannot for the life of you think of the name of your Member of the European Parliament. You have several – each region of the UK has between three and ten. For example, if you live in Cambridge, you have seven MEPs and they all represent you.

The European Parliament may seem distant and not to have much power. But on some issues – Economic Partnerships Agreements, for example – it is useful to lobby your MEP.

To find out who are your MEPs, ring 020 7227 4300, or go to www.europarl.org.uk/uk_meps/MembersMain.htm
Your MEP's address can be found on this website.

Your MP can be reached at:
House of Commons, London SW1A 0AA. Or if you can find your MP's home address, you can send it to there.

Two

Raising awareness of the issues

26. Wear the Make Poverty History white band.

If you watched the BBC's *Vicar of Dibley* programme on New Year's Day 2005, you watched the actors stunned by poverty into wearing Make Poverty History white bands.

The white bands have since become hot property. Oxfam shops started selling them in early January 2005. By early June some 3.6 million had been sold – and Oxfam had ordered 5 million more!

Wearing the white band is your visible personal message that you want poverty to be stopped. You can wear it in a number of ways:

- Around your wrist
- Around your rear view mirror
- As a hair band
- Through the laces in your trainers
- Around the straps of your handbag
- As a lapel ribbon
- On your key ring
- Even on pet collars

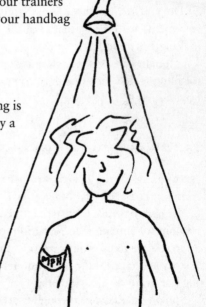

The really important thing is that you wear it! And buy a bundle for your friends. The white bands can be purchased for £1 in Oxfam shops, by post, by telephone and online from several agencies. Or you can add variety by making your own.

Wear the band

every time you walk out of the house, and carry on wearing it.

Action Aid sells a fairly traded white band
(www.actionaid.org).
Also, Art Works for Africa
(www.oxfordfairtrade.org.uk).

27. Flash your white band and start conversations.

If you've got it, flaunt it! Make sure that you flash your band. It can be a great icebreaker and lead to all sorts of conversations about making poverty history.

I was standing in a queue, white band visible on my wrist, and a young woman came up to me and said, 'Do you mind telling me where you got your wristband?'

'From an Oxfam shop', I replied, 'and you can buy them online'.

'Do you realize those wristbands have became a fashion statement,' said the woman. For the first time in my life, I was making a fashion statement!

I thought of the right answer at around 3.00 am the following morning – that fashions may come and go, and it's time for poverty to go.

28. Network like you've never networked before.

Networks, say the cynics, are usually more net than work. Many of us have been there!

Yet networks are there to be used effectively. The Internet is a boom for spreading information to a great many people.

So resolve to use your networks to spread the make poverty history message. Make sure your networking is not only working but firing on all cylinders!

Spread the message through every network you have – your

circle of friends, your church, school, college, hall, place of work, everyone you're in contact with.

Ask people in your network to start their own network on making poverty history. It could all give a new meaning to networking!

29. Organize a Make Poverty History meeting in your area and plan action with others.

Get together with people who also care about making poverty history and organize a local meeting. Make sure that the venue is well-known and easily accessible. Publicize the meeting with churches, local newspapers and radio. Put up posters all over the place.

Involve a number of people as speakers. One could outline the need for the campaign, another could say what people can do. You could show some make poverty history visuals.

Make the meeting fun! You could, for example, include a white band fashion show. Have your volunteer models parade on stage or down the isles wearing a different type of band.

Make sure the meeting ends with plans for action. Circulate a piece of paper, a list and ask everyone to put down their addresses, e-mails, etc. The people at the meeting will be a new network. Keep people up-to-date with news of the issues.

30. Be a media guerrilla. Use phone, fax, snail-mail, e-mail, newsletters or whatever to spread information. Make yourself heard so loudly at your local newspaper, it may well offer you a job.

Blank pages – that's what editors of your local newspaper have before them when they start putting together the paper for the day or the week. They have to fill those pages. You're an obliging sort of person – you want to help. So tell them what you're doing to make poverty history.

When the paper prints what you are doing, you are getting the message across to hundreds or even thousands of people. For a start, make sure you're reading the paper and know how it treats stories. Find the editor's name, the news editor's name. Then e-mail, fax, snail-mail – all three does no harm – a punchy, pithy press release. Follow up with a phone call to ask if they have received it, do they have any queries, will they use it?

Make sure your name and telephone number are prominent on what you send in. Don't forget the letters to the editor column.

Remember that newspapers are interested in what's new. So make sure you are thinking of new activities that could provide a good story and pictures. Invite the editor to your activities, ask her or him to send a photographer along, if appropriate. But have a camera with you just in case. Keep up a steady stream of news to the paper. Imprint yourself on the editor's mind. They will not use everything you send in. But you could have an influence on their policy.

The e-mail, telephone and fax number of your paper should all be prominent in its pages. And include the local radio station in your media activity. Take part in phone-ins if it has them.

31. Speak to your church council about the issues.

Talk to the minister of your church about the issues and ask if you can have a spot on the agenda of your next church council meeting.

Church councils are made up of many different kinds of people. Many members will be there because they care about spiritual and social matters, for others it will be for administration matters. While most will have heard of the Make Poverty History campaign and will be concerned about poverty, not all may be aware of the issues. So do not assume too much knowledge.

Keep your talk free of jargon and include some humour.

Have some specific ideas for what they can do. If you are nervous about speaking to your own church council, ask someone from another church to speak.

32. Ask if you can preach on the issues, or encourage your minister to preach.

The next step is to preach or encourage your minister to do so. There is plenty of guidance should you need it.

The worship section of the Christian Aid website (www.christian-aid.org.uk/worship/reflect/reflect.htm) has reflections on many topics, including:

- The Sermon on the Mount
- Where faith and politics meet

- Looking after the children of the future
- Peace as the fruit of justice
- From the desert may bloom justice and peace
- Repent . . . and campaign; how we might bring about change.

Lectionary readings with suggested themes and links to development statistics and stories can be accessed on: www.bathwells.anglican.org/mission/wm_linked_lectionary. php.

Or you may prefer to prepare something entirely original on God's concern for the poor. It helps to dramatize your message. You will get the immediate attention of the congregation, for example, if you begin by saying you would like to divide them into three groups. Ask Group 1 to shout 'One!' with you, Group 2, 'Two!', Group 3, 'Three!' Then say, 'In the three seconds we have done that, if those three seconds were typical, a child will have died of poverty.'

Urge the congregation to put their hearts on the side of the world's poorest. After the service, mingle and be ready for questions. And encourage people to become active.

33. Organize a Make Poverty History service in your area.

Invite a number of churches to participate in this. Ask your local Churches Together team to work with you in organizing a Make Poverty History service. Involve university or college chaplains if appropriate. Speak with your local Christian Aid organizer.

Both the Christian Aid and Cafod websites have suggestions for appropriate forms of worship. Adapt to your own needs. Choose appropriate hymns and readings, perhaps ranging wider than the Bible. You could include readings from prominent Christians, for example.

For the venue, choose a church in a central location. Choose readers from every local church. Make sure that no one is left out!

Ask someone who is either well-known or from a developing country to preach. Have a questions and answers sessions after her or his sermon. Have a spot at the end when you inform people about local activities.

34. Hang a large MAKEPOVERTYHISTORY banner in your area.

It is time to let Make Poverty History all hang out. Or rather to hang up a large banner on your local church, meeting room, town hall, sports centre, school, college or wherever.

It will make passers-by think if the next time they walk down the High Street they see a large banner reading: MAKEPOVERTYHISTORY.

You can always make your own banner. But a North of England-based company is making white vinyl banners 12 foot long and 18 inches deep, with the wording MAKEPOVERTYHISTORY. The banners have eyelets every 2 feet and cost £39–80.

Weigh up the most prominent position in your area to hang the banner. And have some leaflets available nearby so that people can enquire what it's all about.

Tell your local press that you have put up the banner and why. Ask them to come and take a picture.

NB: You will, of course, need permission to hang up a banner. And you will need someone with experience of these things to actually hang the banner.

Express Banners Ltd, 290 Chorley New Road, Horwich BL6 5NY; tel: 01204 698787;
www.jdc-web.org.uk/wdm/WDM-Resources.htm

35. Hold a discussion group to consider what Judaism, Christianity and Islam have to say on God's concern for the poor.

God's special concern for the poor is seen many times in the Old Testament, the New Testament and The Koran.

In the Old Testament, God is the liberator of the oppressed (Exodus 20:2; Deuteronomy 5:6). The psalmist speaks of 'defending the fatherless and the oppressed' (10:18a). 'The Lord has anointed me to preach good news to the poor,' says the prophet Isaiah (61:1b). 'Do not exploit the poor because they are poor, and do not crush the needy in court,' warns the writer of Proverbs (22:22).

In the New Testament, Jesus begins his ministry with the words: 'The spirit of the Lord is upon me because he has anointed me to preach good news to the poor . . . to release the oppressed, to proclaim the year of the Lords favour' (Luke 4:18–19).

The Koran says: 'God has permitted trading and made usury unlawful' (The Cow 2:275). 'Greedily you lay your hands on the inheritance of the weak and you love riches with all your hearts' (The Dawn, 89:20).

Questions for discussion

1. Read Leviticus 25:8–17. The Year of Jubilee was intended to give everyone a fresh start, no matter how poor they had

become. Is Jubilee needed for our time? Should usury, interest on loans, be unlawful? Could Judaism, Christianity and Islam unite to press the case for Jubilee?

2. Consider Micah 6:8: 'What does the Lord require of you? To act justly and love mercy.' What does the Lord require of us today? (see www.micahchallenge.org)

3. The Bible and the Koran both warn against greed. Examine how greed can contribute to poverty.

36. Bring the issue before your deanery, diocesan or national church synods/meetings/conferences/assemblies.

The local level is fine but also spread the message wider. The mainstream churches all have regional assemblies that meet periodically and which are attended by people from a wider area.

In the Church of England, for example, the diocesan synod meets about three times a year and might be attended by some 200 people. A diocese may cover three counties and will have a Board for Social Responsibility. Speak to the chairman and ask if she or he would support a motion on making poverty history.

If you are not a member of the synod, you will need to get a member to move the motion.

Ask the diocesan bishop if he would speak and support it. As bishops are a unifying force, it's good to have him with you. A diocesan synod can forward a motion to the General Synod which has over 600 members from the whole of the UK.

The local, district and national type of structure is common to most churches. The Methodist Church, for example, is organized into circuits and districts with the national Conference as its the governing body.

Enter the name of your church into a search engine and find out about its structure.

37. Hand out leaflets on making poverty history in shopping areas.

When people push their trolleys through supermarket checkouts, they have before them half the world. The coffee, the nuts, the sugar may have come from Africa, the tea, the rice, the spices from Asia, etc., etc.

But many of the products in their trolley will have been produced by people in developing countries for a pittance.

So prepare a leaflet to hand out in shopping areas. Word it carefully and politely. Point out that many of the goods in their trolley could not be grown in Britain. We are dependent on the poor to produce our tea, coffee, etc. for us. Ask – don't the growers deserve a decent return?

Tell the press what you are doing and ask them to send a photographer along.

38. Dramatize the message – organize street theatre.

When something different happens along the high street, people stop and take notice. So make the different happen – organize some street theatre on a make poverty history theme.

Street theatre has been called the 'Rock and Roll of Performing Arts'. For a start it's inclusive – crossing generations and social groups. It is usually a short and attention-grabbing drama that can either have words or be silent. If you have friends with drama skills you could write and stage something yourself. You may have an amateur dramatic society near you that is willing to co-operate.

For example, you could stage a football match with one team carrying heavy weights on their legs and with the goalie blindfolded. The referee – with WTO in large letters on his back – is hugely biased against this weaker side!

You could do a sketch in which a man tries to get out of a

straitjacket. He wriggles and wrestles, he strains and stretches, but nothing seems to happen. (See www.pressureworks.org. uk/tradejustice/latest/straitjacket.html)

You could hold the street theatre in a set place – if it's a shopping centre you may need permission – or you can make it a walking drama. You could, for example, stage a funeral procession through the streets to highlight how the government's free trade agenda is killing communities and livelihoods in developing countries.

The Bananas is a professional silent street theatre group that performed in London in Trade Justice Week in April 2005 (www.theatreofadventure.co.uk).

Credo Arts Community (www.credoartscommunity.org.uk)

has produced a booklet with 17 ideas for street theatre with trade justice themes.

39. Organize a rich world–poor world meal.

'Chicken for MP – mayor gets rice' ran the headline in a local paper. It was reporting on a rich world–poor world meal in the town. This kind of meal is a parable of the world – and it makes for a fun evening!

Get a small team together, choose a venue, print tickets and do some publicity. Invite the MP, the mayor, etc. Tell people from the start exactly what they will be coming to – an evening when a third of diners can expect a three-course meal and two-thirds a bowl of rice.

Make it clear that people will have no idea which meal they will receive until they arrive. Spread the cooking as widely as possible, organize some music and a speaker.

When people arrive, they draw a ticket, marked either rich or poor. The rich ticket-holders walk up to beautifully laid-out tables with fine cutlery, wine glasses, etc. The poor ticket-holders go to bare tables.

The rich get their starter while the poor sit and watch. The rich may gather up a few crumbs from their starter course – and take them over to the poor.

The poor are given their rice when the rich have their main course. The poor may like to approach the tables of the rich and ask for say half a carrot, a symbol of the 0.7 per cent aid target.

The rich are served with their pudding while the poor sit around, sensing the injustice of it all, even seeking asylum on the tables of the rich.

Meal over, the speaker stresses that it does not have to be like this. You could then draw the parable to a close – and serve everyone fair trade coffee.

40. Devise a make poverty history exhibition. Ask local schools, your local library to take it for a period.

Schools and libraries often have exhibitions. These present a good opportunity to spread the message. Get a group of people together and devise an attention-grabbing exhibition on making poverty history.

You can download images from www.makepovertyhistory. org and ask Christian Aid, Cafod, etc. for posters. Keep a balance between showing poverty as it is, and also showing the hope.

If you can make it secure, you could set up a laptop computer with a make poverty history presentation that automatically changes images every minute or whatever time you decide. Again you can download images for a PowerPoint presentation from www.makepovertyhistory.org.

Make sure there is a pad for people to write down their name and address if they would like more information.

**41. Ask to speak at school assembles and to local organiza-
tions.**

Find out who is responsible for running assemblies at the
different schools in your area. Offer to talk about making
poverty history. Teachers who run assemblies are often pleased
to have new ideas and someone coming in to give a talk.

Large schools may have their own radio programme. Ask
if you can be interviewed. Make what you say punchy and
clear, don't talk down, but don't assume too much knowledge
either.

Local organizations that meet regularly have to find a
constant stream of new people for their yearly programmes.
Rotary Clubs, Mothers Union branches, Women's Institutes,
etc. all need speakers on interesting topics. Your local library
will have a list of organizations in your area. Write or other-
wise contact them and offer to arrange a speaker.

It is a good idea to have a small team of speakers as some
organizations meet in the day, others in the evenings.

**42. Do a walk or bike ride to publicize the issues, handing out
leaflets en-route.**

Take the make poverty history message out on foot or by bike.
In One World Week, October 2004, I cycled the TransPennine
Way, from Southport on the Irish Sea to Hornsea near Hull on
the North Sea, to raise awareness of a campaign that was soon
to be launched – Make Poverty History.

I carried leaflets with me about the campaign and handed
them to people whenever I could. I stayed with friends a couple of nights and one of them organized an evening meeting for
me to talk about the campaign to a local group. Another day I
was interviewed on a school's radio programme.

The ride was 230 miles and took four days. You can, of
course, organize any length.

Cycling or walking also enables you to make the point that if our world is to have a future we need to lower our emissions of carbon dioxide, end our love affair with the motor car and stop polluting the atmosphere. And, again, tell the press what you are doing.

43. Organize a Make Poverty History walk around churches in your area, handing out leaflets en-route.

In some areas, churches get together on Good Friday and organize a walk around them all, and also take in the town/city centre. This type of walk can be organized any time. It has a double appeal.

First, it can attract the support and added commitment of people from the different churches. Second, shoppers etc. will see the walk and maybe take a leaflet you are handing out. You could organize some music – drums, for example – and perhaps have a few people dressed in highly colourful costume. It all helps to attract attention! You could combine some street theatre on the move with the walk.

Make prayer an important part. Begin and end the walk with prayer, pray outside each church you visit and at other strategic points.

Inform the police of your plans. You may need to get their permission.

44. Hold a sleep-out, an all-night vigil in your town.

Sleeping out all night, keeping a vigil, is another way of attracting attention and publicity for the cause. It's not for everyone and is more likely to attract young people. You could sleep outside in the open air or in a church.

There are a number of things you can include in the vigil. Cafod has prepared a vigil service for Make Poverty History.

This can be accessed on:

www.cafod.org.uk/resources/worship/liturgies_and_
services/parish_liturgies/mph_vigil

You could follow up the service by breaking into groups to discuss some of the implications of the message you have heard, and how it might inspire you in your activities.

At some stage in the night – get some sleep!

A successful vigil for trade justice was held in April 2005 when at least 25,000 people spent the night in and around central London (details on the Christian Aid website).

Take full advantage of the press opportunities this offers. Tell the press what you are doing and why. Invite them to take pictures.

45. Hold a multicultural carnival.

Organize a carnival that celebrates different cultures in music, drama and dance – it's ambitious but it will attract attention! Such carnivals have featured in many university rag weeks.

So get together with a wide range of people and consider organizing a carnival with a Make Poverty History theme. Talk with church ministers and leaders in your area, also community groups. Involve chaplaincies, local schools, plan a colourful procession, book music groups.

Plan well-ahead, choose a summer date, organize competitions, such as spoken-word and creative-writing competitions for different age groups. Organize prizes for the best float. Talk with the police about the route.

For ideas, look at the website of Europe's biggest carnival, the Notting Hill. The theme of this carnival in 2004 was 'Freedom and Justice' (www.lnhc.org.uk).

Also see www.lusu.co.uk/green/oww for details of a 'multicultural carnival of celebration and reconciliation' that Lancaster University students held in 2004.

If organizing your own carnival is too ambitious, look into

the possibility of having a Make Poverty History exhibition/ presentation at an existing event. This has been a feature of the annual WOMAD (World of Music, Arts & Dance) festival in Reading.

46. Organize an event in your area in the annual One World Week (the last week in October).

One World Week is a development education programme established by churches in 1978. It's an annual opportunity to join a wide movement of people taking action for justice locally and globally. It offers an excellent opportunity for groups concerned with these issues to promote events.

Each year the week has a different theme. The 2005 theme was 'Promises, promises, make poverty history'. Politicians have made their promises, now let's see they keep them.

Every year in One World Week over a thousand local events typically take place. The emphasis is on action at the local level. The aim is to further the cause of justice at the global level.

Go to www.oneworldweek.org to view the vast range of events taking place – and for ideas! Among the resources listed on the site is an Ecumenical Worship Anthology – 'Resources for Christian worship in One World Week'.

47. Make it fun!

Poverty is literally a deadly business. In the task of raising awareness of the issues, you do have to communicate just how serious it is, a child dying every three seconds.

But in the way you communicate the issues, you need to strike a balance. Talk about the poverty but speak also of the hope. Take the issues seriously but campaign on them in a way that people will find attractive. And it will be attractive if you make it fun. If you are mournful and downcast, people will hardly be inspired to join you. Look for the humour, the pathos in the issue, and use it when you speak.

Many of the ideas in this section lend themselves to making it fun – street theatre, walks, carnivals, etc. If people can see something in your campaigning which is attractive despite the problems, you are more likely to have them come and join you.

Three

Getting to know more

48. Read more on development issues.

In 1970 I asked a university professor/development campaigner, 'Suppose I have £50 to spend on tackling poverty – what's the best place for my money?'

Without hesitation he replied, 'Invest the bulk of it in new books on poverty.' To tackle poverty, it helps to know as much as you can about poverty. And it pays to keep up-to-date, with new research and case studies, the latest insights.

Ask at a good bookshop for their latest lists on poverty and development. Some publishers, Zed Books for example, publish only books on development (www.zedbooks.co.uk).

Read widely – books by authors with different viewpoints but the same goal, the end of poverty; books that are both pro and anti-globalization, books on the World Trade Organization, etc.

Some people feel it's good not to buy a newspaper and so cut down on the paper that's used. But if you don't buy newspapers, at least read them online or in libraries (see below). Take out a subscription to development-related magazines such as the monthly *New Internationalist*. This exists 'to report on the issues of world poverty and inequality'. It also publishes a range of No-Nonsense guides to development issues (www. newint.org).

If you are going to tackle politicians about poverty issues you need to know as much as they do – and more! Then you're more likely to see the flaws in their arguments. So it's vital to keep up to speed with what is going on.

49. Join member-based development agencies.

Becoming a member of a development agency makes you part of a wider, national network committed to the cause of making poverty history.

Set up in 1969, the World Development Movement, (WDM) does not fund development projects but rather 'tackles the root causes of world poverty'. It campaigns for fairer world trade, regulating transnational corporations, cancelling debt, and more and better aid. WDM lobbies decision-makers to change the policies that keep people poor. With 15,000 supporters and campaigners in 70 groups around the UK, the WDM claims to be 'one of the UK's most dynamic campaigning organizations', with some major campaign successes. Membership costs £16 a year (www.wdm.org.uk).

War on Want was set up in 1953. It fights poverty in developing countries in partnership and solidarity with people affected by globalization. It campaigns for workers' rights 'and against the root causes of global poverty, inequality and injustice'. Membership costs £15 a year (www.waronwant.org).

Friends of the Earth has its roots in the environment but campaigns on related development issues – calling, for example, for regulation of transnational corporations. Membership costs £36 a year (www.foe.co.uk).

SPEAK, the prayer and campaigns network for students and young people, is a free membership organization (www.speak.org.uk).

Christian Aid and Cafod have supporters rather than members and again you can be part of their activity by logging on, in the first instance, to the sites as listed in section 23 above.

50. Read the newspapers of developing countries – readily accessible online.

On the day I'm writing this, I learned soon after breakfast that:

- Dominica will not survive in the global economy if the Caribbean island's annual growth rate does not double, according to a government minister.
- 39,000 textile manufacturing jobs are likely to be lost in Kenya following the end of quotas in a US–Africa agreement called the African Growth and Opportunity Act.
- Bangladesh and Vietnam have agreed to expand and strengthen bilateral co-operation in trade, investment, agriculture, banking, education and sports 'for the benefit of the two peoples'.

From where did I glean this and a great deal more? From *The Paper Boy*, one of the 'favourite' sites on my computer. By logging on to www.thepaperboy.com I have access to over 6,000 online newspapers – from every country in the world. Free.

Thanks to the Internet it is now easy to read the newspapers of developing countries, and to look at the broad range of development news – usually far more in-depth than in western country papers. To read all of them you would, of course, have to be an exceptional linguist – as well as needing rather more than 24 hours a day! But papers in English make up a good proportion.

And if you want to read all the stories from around the world on a particular issue – trade, for example – register the key word as an 'alert' with a search engine such as Google and you can receive a daily listing.

51. Make friends with someone of another race, ethnicity or economic background.

Many of us move, live and work within a rather small circle. The people we went to school with, or work with, go to church with, campaign with to make poverty history, they may well have a similar background to ourselves.

So go out of your way to make friends with someone of another race, ethnicity or economic background. You might start in your own street or place of work! Or join an organization that attracts people of all races, ethnicities and backgrounds. If there is a development education centre in your area, it may be worth asking for their advice.

Spend time with a new friend, ask questions, listen to their answers. Their perspective, their views, may be very different from yours. If your new friend is an immigrant she or he may well have far more first-hand experience of poverty – and be more angry about it. Such friendships can deepen understanding and awareness.

52. While travel by air is best avoided, because of its demands on fuel, holidaying in a developing country can increase understanding of poverty. But make it an 'alternative' holiday, staying with a local family.

Living with the poor will give you an insight into poverty and development that you cannot get from books, newspapers or television programmes. It could sadden and anger you, fire and inspire you, change your view of poverty and strengthen your determination to make it history.

Taking a standard package tour will not help much. And it's best to avoid flying if you can. The aviation industry is set to become the number one culprit for greenhouse gas emissions.

What you can do is take an alternative holiday. Hundreds of

them are now available. And go overland if you have the time. Both Africa and Asia can be reached overland with just a short journey over sea.

Tourism Concern publishes a book which lists alternatives. It has details of travel operators that offer holidays where you can stay with a family in the heart of a community.

And if you are healthy and young – of whatever age – consider offering yourself for voluntary service in a developing country.

The Good Alternative Travel Guide (Mark Mann, Tourism Concern/Earthscan, £9.99).
Details on www.tourismconcern.org.uk
VSO (Voluntary Service Overseas) www.vso.org.uk
GAP, www.gapyear.com

53. Join Make Poverty History and check the site regularly for new information, events etc.

By joining Make Poverty History you add your weight to the campaign, and the website is a mine of information. You can view the latest news relating to the campaign, a listing of the main events, and events in your area. You can register the events you are planning and look at what's happening outside the UK. And there's a list of videos to watch.

Some of the events you may know about, others may have escaped your attention.

And check for who has joined. By July 2005, 500 organizations had become part of the campaign – a doubling in two months. New ones join almost every day. Check the list and if an organization has joined and someone you know is a member it – tell them. They may not have heard!

www.makepovertyhistory.org

Four

Unleashing your purchasing power

54. Buy and enjoy the growing range of Fairtrade certified foods.

Revolution just about describes it. In 1970 they did not exist. At the start of the third millennium a mere handful of Fairtrade certified foods were available. By early 2005 there were 350 Fairtrade certified retail products in the UK, mostly foodstuffs. And what a range!

Coffee, tea, sugar, chocolate, drinking chocolate, pasta, rice, muesli, fruit juice, honey, marmalade, jams, fruit and nuts, biscuits and snacks were available. And all the supermarket chains now stock them.

Under the Fairtrade system, producers normally organize into groups (there's a different system for plantation workers) and receive a guaranteed price which covers the cost of production and allows for investment and a living wage. The Fairtrade Foundation awards the FAIRTRADE Mark to products which meet internationally recognized standards.

Foods with the FAIRTRADE Mark are now sold in 17 countries through 235 traders and 452 companies. They come from 360 producer groups in 36 countries, representing 5 million growers and their families. It adds up to a real difference to the lives of millions of the poorest.

So join the revolution! Every time you buy a Fairtrade certified food you are helping someone to edge out of poverty. It's a great way of using your power as a shopper. And organize a special event in your area in Fairtrade Fortnight, the first two weeks in March, or on World Fair Trade Day which is held each year on 14 May.

The Fairtrade Foundation (www.fairtrade.org.uk).

55. Drink Fairtrade wine and fruit juice.

When a severe earthquake struck the wine-growing Curicó Valley, south of the Chilean capital Santiago, it was as always poorer growers who were the worst affected.

To help rebuild peoples lives, a co-operative called Los Robles linked up with the UK supermarket chain, the Co-op to produce the first supermarket Fairtrade certified wine. Not only did growers receive a fair price for their grapes, the community also benefited from a social fund that invested in healthcare, housing and irrigation.

Fairtrade wine from South Africa as well as Chile is now on the shelves, not only of the Co-op but also of other major supermarkets. Thandi Fairtrade wine from South Africa won a gold medal at London's International Wine Challenge 2004.

Most of the cartons of fruit juice on shop shelves are orange juice. And most of the oranges in the cartons are grown on plantations by seasonal workers who struggle to get decent wages and conditions. Fairtrade juice is the alternative.

Look for the Fruit Passion and JP Juices brand of Fairtrade juices. Both come from co-operatives in Cuba.

Serving fairly traded wine and fruit juice at parties is a great way to engage people in the issues.

56. Clothe yourself with fair trade.

There is no need to wear clothes produced in sweatshops. Fairly trade clothes are not only available, they are also fashionable.

People Tree is a pioneer in fair trade fashion. Working in partnership with 70 producer groups in 20 Asian, African and Latin American countries, it offers a wide range of organic cotton and handwoven fabrics made by 'some of the world's most marginalized communities'. It provides product design skills and assistance, a fair price, regular orders and advance payment as needed. It also supports village welfare projects and schools for the children of producers (www.ptree.co.uk).

One of the UK's oldest fair trade companies, Traidcraft, lists a wide rage of fashion clothes in its catalogue – including cardigans from Nepal, pistachio T-shirts and vests from Mauritius, skirts and summer jackets from India, check shirts from Bangladesh and T-shirts from Zimbabwe. Traidcraft says that it only sources clothing that uses chemical-free dyes, natural dyes 'or items made from organic cotton' (www.traidcraft. co.uk)

The British Association of Fair Trade Shops lists a number of members who sell clothing online or by e-mail: www.bafts. org.uk/buy_fair_trade_epost.asp?reg=Mail%20Order%20an d%20Internet

So ditch the designer labels – and clothe yourself with fair trade!

57. Publicize how fairly traded products help producers to overcome poverty.

Nicaraguan coffee-grower Blanca Rosa Molina farms three hectares of land in the Matagalpa region in the north of the country. A member of a co-operative, Blanca sells about a third of her coffee for the Fairtrade price of US$1.26 a pound – a price substantially higher than in the early years of the twenty-first century.

When I asked Blanca what difference the Fairtrade system makes to her, she was clear: 'The difference that Fairtrade makes is that we know we shall eat tomorrow.'

Regina Joseph grows bananas on her two and a half acre plot of sloping land in Dominica, one of the four Windward Islands in eastern Caribbean. Before linking up with the Fairtrade system in 1999, Regina was paid a pittance for her fruit. Today she receives a living return.

'Fairtrade has transformed the lives of small farmers,' Regina told me. 'We used to get US$2 for an 18-kilo box of bananas, a very low price that often did not allow us to send our children to school or to put shoes on their feet. Now we are selling Fairtrade certified bananas and getting a good price – US$5.75 a box. This makes a huge difference.'

Publicize real-life stories like this! Use the above if you wish, and you will find more on the Fairtrade Foundation website (www.fairtrade.org.uk).

58. If you shop at a supermarket, write to the manager to ask that more Fairtrade products are stocked.

The supermarket nearest to you is likely to stock some Fairtrade products. But you would like it to stock more. Find out the name of the manager and write to her or him and say so. Enclose a list of the products that are available – not all 350, just the general product – mangoes, fruit juice, etc.

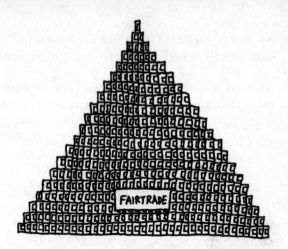

The manager may reply that the branch would like to stock more Fairtrade certified products but that shelf space is limited. Reply with figures that show the growth – that sales of certified Fairtrade products in British shops rose from £60 million in 2002 to £93 million in 2003 and to £140 million in 2004.

Point out how the growth shows that shoppers are increasingly demanding Fairtrade products and want to see more on the shelves.

If you're successful, the next step is to keep those goods there – or rather to buy them and encourage others to buy them so that the manager keeps them there! Follow-up is therefore essential. If the goods don't sell, the branch will cease to stock them.

In addition, you might also ask coffee shops and restaurants in your area to offer fairly traded products. The FairTrade Foundation has 'order up' cards that you can hand in to help do this.

59. Become a Fair Trader and organize a Fairtrade stall in your church, school, university, etc. on a regular basis.

All over Britain they are trading, not to make money for themselves but to help beat poverty. Under a scheme run by Traidcraft, some 5,000 people have become Fair Traders in the UK.

Fair Traders are volunteers who:

- sell Fairtrade products from stalls at their church, school, university or at local events;
- pass catalogues to family and friends and collect orders;
- organize parties at home.

New Fair Traders receive a start-up kit of promotional and display items, including catalogues, a point of sale unit, degradable carrier bags, pricing gun labels, Fair Trader event invitation cards, and a Traidcraft car window sticker. Fair Traders keep some stock at home and order new stock from Traidcraft as needed. In some areas, an established Fair Trader can lend experience and support.

If you are thinking of starting a stall in your church, decide the frequency – say once a month after the main service – and secure permission from the church council. Should anyone say – and it's happened – that Jesus threw the money-changers out of the temple, and that a church should not be a market place, remind them that Jesus threw them out because they were cheating the poor. Fair trade is the complete opposite – it's all about benefiting the poor. When the church – people – uses its shell – a building – to benefit the poor, that glorifies God.

To find out more about becoming a Fair Trader, ring Traidcraft, 0191 497 6417, e-mail jeanc@traidcraft.co.uk, or complete an online registration form at www.traidcraft. co.uk.

Tearcraft (www.tearcraft.co.uk) runs a similar scheme.

60. Urge your church to become a Fairtrade church, using only Fairtrade goods at church functions.

Be part of a growing trend. Lay a resolution before your church council that only Fairtrade goods are served at church functions. Start by proposing just the tea and coffee if you favour a step-by-step approach.

Church functions will, of course, include not just the coffee after a service but patronal festival celebrations, summer fêtes, etc.

Ask the council to complement this by developing the church's witness to the poor through prayer, study and further action. As part of the action, suggest to the council that it submits a resolution to the diocesan synod or regional assembly that the diocese or region goes Fairtrade.

In the Church of England, Chester became the first Fairtrade diocese in 2003. Others have followed. Chester diocese now runs courses on Fairtrade (www.chester.anglican.org/fairtrade). In the Roman Catholic Church, Portsmouth diocese led the way (www.portsmouth-dio.org.uk/pp/04_03/10_soc_resp.htm). The Witney and Faringdon Circuit (Oxfordshire) was the first Methodist circuit to go fully Fairtrade.

And think wider still. Churches in the north-east of England are working with Local Action 21 in Durham and Christian Aid to encourage the North East to become a Fairtrade region. The United Reform Church plays a key role is this initiative (www.northeastchurches.org.uk/project.php?catid=9).

It only needs a small number of people committed to justice to get things moving.

61. Hold a Fairtrade breakfast, lunch or supper in your home or church.

This is a good way to get people together to sample some of the growing range of Fairtrade products. More and more people today are familiar with Fairtrade tea and coffee. Some people may tell you that they tried the coffee in the 1970s and didn't like it. Ask them to try it again. Today's Fairtrade certified coffee bears absolutely no relation!

Many people may not be aware of other Fairtrade products – fruit juice, muesli, marmalade, honey, sugar – all breakfast table items.

For lunch and supper there's pasta, rice, sauces, nuts and raisins, spices and herbs. Make sure you have a Fairtrade stall where people can buy the items they like. Have some leaflets around and perhaps arrange for a short talk while people are eating. And, whatever you do, make it fun.

62. Press for your locality to become a Fairtrade town or borough.

What do Garstang, Aberdeen, Cardiff, York, Hereford, Bristol, Oxford and Lewes have in common? All of them are Fairtrade towns.

Garstang in Lancashire deserves pride of place because in May 2000 it declared itself the world's first Fairtrade town. This caught the imagination of local people and the interest of politicians. And it made headlines across the north-west of England – hugely raising awareness of Fairtrade in the area.

To become a Fairtrade town – there are now well over a hundred – five goals must be met, the Fairtrade Foundation says.

1 The local council must pass a resolution supporting

Fairtrade, and serve Fairtrade coffee and tea at its meetings and in offices and canteens.

2 A range of Fairtrade products must be readily available in the area's shops and served in local cafés and catering establishments.

3 Fairtrade products must be used by a number of local work places (estate agents, hairdressers, etc.) and community organizations (churches, schools, etc.).

4 The council must attract popular support for the campaign.

5 A local Fairtrade steering group must be convened to ensure continued commitment to Fairtrade town status.

You may have some work to do to ensure that your town qualifies. Then talk to a local councillor who is sympathetic.

To apply, and find out more, download the Fairtrade Town Goals and Action Guide and application form (www.fairtrade. org.uk). You can also view the full list of Fairtrade towns and those working towards it. You can order a hard copy from the Fairtrade Foundation, 16 Baldwin's Gardens, London ECIN 7RJ, tel: 020 7405 5952.

63. Hold a Fairtrade fashion show in your town.

Over a hundred curious shoppers sat down at a Buckinghamshire church on a Saturday for a fashion show with a difference.

At Christ Church in Flackwell Heath the audience witnessed Fairtrade clothes paraded by on the 'catwalk'. Three companies, Traidcraft, Toybox Charity and the Nepal Leprosy Trust, all staged their own catwalk collections, And while models changed for the following collection, a video was shown of their work with Third World producers.

At the end of the show – over a complimentary glass of Fairtrade wine – shoppers were given the all-important information about where Fairtrade clothing could be purchased locally.

So stage your own fashion show. Choose a church or hall in a busy shopping area, talk to Traidcraft and other companies and recruit some volunteer models. And ensure that the clothes are available locally.

Traidcraft (www.traidcraft.co.uk)
Toybox Charity (www.toyboxcharity.org.uk)
Nepal Leprosy Trust (www.nlt.org.uk)

64. Give Fairtrade products as Christmas, birthday presents, etc.

Solve the problem of what to give at Christmas, birthdays and other occasions by delving into the Fairtrade catalogues!

From the Traidcraft catalogue you can choose items you may never have given before, such as foot massagers from India, stone-etched paperweights from Bangladesh, banana trees from Thailand. At the more traditional end, there's Fairtrade chocolate and wine, plus a wide range of fashion goods.

From the People Tree catalogue there are handwoven silk dresses and skirts from a village near Calcutta, ceramic tableware from Vietnam, plus clothes, accessories and jewellery.

If you prefer to shop in person, Oxfam has 750 shops in the UK with a attractive range of gifts, including Christmas cards.

Or you can do something really different – give a goat! Well, actually you give a goat – or a chicken, even a donkey – in someone's name and it goes to a family in a developing country. Charities such as Oxfam and Harvest Help report huge interest in this. It's a novel way of giving a present that can make a contribution towards making poverty history.

Traidcraft (www.traidcraft.co.uk)
Tel: 00191 491 0591

People Tree (www.peopletree.co.uk)
Tel: 0845 450 4595
Oxfam (www.oxfam.org.uk)
Tel: 01865 311311

Harvest Help (www.harvesthelp.org)
Tel: 01952 260699

65. Don't buy products made by companies that you believe are acting irresponsibly in developing countries. Boycotts work.

Companies selling goods and services depend on people buying them for their survival. A boycott, refusing to buy specific products, is capable of bringing changes in policy.

Boycotts work! They have at least modified the behaviour of some companies. They cost them money. A Co-operative Bank survey found that consumer boycotts cost big brands $2.5 billion a year – compared to retail sales of $230 billion.

The most astonishing change in corporate policy in recent years came in the late 1990s when UK shoppers refused to buy genetically modified foods. This led to a major – and speedy – change in the policies of the giant food retail corporations and fast food chains.

McDonald's, Exxon-Mobil, Shell and Nestlé are among companies that have attracted consumer boycotts. There have been significant successes. An investment bank warned Exxon-Mobil, for example, that being tarred with the label 'environmental enemy number one' is a risk to its business.

The Rainforest Action Network called off its long-standing boycott of Mitsubishi in 2000 after two of its companies signed an agreement with the Alliance committing themselves to making changes to their wood and paper purchasing policies. This signalled a victory for the campaign to promote more responsible forestry practices.

It is the bottom line that matters for the companies: 'We don't fear regulation, what we fear is customer revolt,' admitted a Shell official (quoted in Anita Roddick, *Take it Personally*, Element Books 2003, p. 30), So revolt when you think it's necessary.

Ethical Consumer – an organization that looks at the social and environmental records of the companies behind brand names – publishes a list of current boycotts in the UK (www. ethicalconsumer.org/boy cotts/boycotts_list.htm).

66. If you have money to invest, choose an ethical plan.

In the 1980s they barely existed. A sign of growing social consciousness is that today there are thousands to choose them – ethical investments.

For starters you could look at Triodos Bank. This guarantees that savings will only be used to finance businesses and charities that benefit people and the environment. And the bank tells you which organizations it lends to. On offer are a range of accounts that connect savings with specific causes that matter to the saver (www.triodos.co.uk).

Shared Interest is a co-operative lending society that aims to reduce poverty by providing fair and just financial services. With some 8,000 members it lends to and works with 'producer and buyer organizations who are committed to using fair trade principles' (www.shared-interest.com).

Jupiter Asset Management has a number of green funds and publishes a Green Guide which explains more about green investments (www.jupiteronline.co.uk).

The Ethical Investment Co-operative is a firm of independent financial advisers specializing in ethical and socially responsible investment (www.ethicalmoney.org).

See also the Ethical Investment Research Service site (www.eiris.org).

Five

Changing the way you live

67. Leave the car in the garage or better still donate it to charity or sell it. Cycle, walk or use public transport.

I cycle to my nearest railway station in a dependable seven minutes. If I went by car it could take me 20 minutes and even longer if the traffic is really bad. The bike is both quicker and more enjoyable.

If you live in an urban area, it's likely that the traffic is getting worse. Those queues that used to form half a mile from the town centre now start a mile away. You will have your own horror stories. Why not leave the car behind and get on your bike?

If you have an old bike, consider trading it in for a new one. It's an investment. Gears and brakes will be better. Resolve that all your journeys in and around town will be by bike. If you live deep in the country, consider buying a fold-up bike. Put it in the back of the car, drive to the outskirts of town and then cycle into the centre.

If you cycle to work, keep a change of clothes there in case it rains. And pray for the day when a genius invents a totally enclosed, rain-proof bike!

If a bike doesn't suit, you could walk if the distance is not too great. Or try the bus. Many services have improved. If a bus can get you to work, to the shops as quickly as a car, you'll become a bus fan. But government policies are hardly encouraging a switch to the bus. Motoring costs fell by 6 per cent in real terms between 1997 and 2004, says Friends of the Earth, whereas the cost of travelling by bus rose over this period (www.foe.co.uk).

68. For long journeys, take the train not the plane or the car.

The European Commission has calculated that an aircraft on a flight of around 500 km has a fuel consumption of 10.5 litres per 100 passenger-km. Trains consume only 2.3 litres per 100 km (3.0 litres per 100 km for high-speed trains): 'For those domestic journeys in the UK which are under this distance (for example, London to Manchester), the benefits of rail may be even greater.'

A car is in the middle of plane and train for environmental impact depending on engine size and speed travelled.

In terms of carbon dioxide emissions, trains score even more heavily. An Intergovernmental Panel on Climate Change report 'Aviation and the Global Atmosphere' shows that short-haul air travel emits up to 98 grams of carbon per passenger-km compared to just under 50 by a high-speed train using coal-fired electricity – less for trains using non-fossil electricity (www.grida.no/climate/ipcc/aviation).

A train will typically carry far more passengers than a plane. If it happens to be four times as many, then per passenger emissions are around eight times more on the plane than the train.

If you're heading for an isolated destination, and you feel a car is essential, take a full load of passengers if you can and so cut down your emissions per person.

Source: 'From Planes to Trains', Aviation Environment Federation for Friends of the Earth, October 2000 (www.foe. co.uk).
To calculate the emissions of a journey by air, go to www. chooseclimate.org.

69. If a car is essential, buy a hybrid vehicle that uses less fuel.

'New "green" car for bishop' read the headline of a church press release. The Bishop of Oxford, the Rt Revd Richard Harries had taken delivery of a car 'which will help to save the planet from greenhouse gases', it said.

The car – a Toyota Prius – is a hybrid which has an electric motor and a petrol engine. The car's electronics automatically run the petrol engine as necessary to keep the battery charged. At low speeds, in towns and cities, the car is powered purely by the electric motor. As the speed climbs, the petrol engine cuts in.

Going hybrid is something to take seriously. In money terms, hybrid vehicles cost more. In terms of cost to the environment, they cost much less.

Diocese of Oxford (www.oxford.anglican.org).

70. Convert your car to run on LPG.

As an alternative to buying a hybrid, consider converting your existing car to run on liquified petroleum gas (LPG).

According to an Energy Saving Trust fact sheet: 'LPG vehicles can significantly reduce the output of key target pollutants . . . as well as contributing to reductions in carbon dioxide emissions.'

Conversion will cost about £1,500 but you will pay only 34p–41p a litre for fuel, compared with over 80p a litre for petrol. Work out how long it would take for you to get your money back, allowing for doing 5–10 per cent fewer miles per gallon than with petrol.

There are two points at least to consider, however. LPG is still a fossil fuel and not sustainable. More immediately you would need to check availability of LPG in your area. Not all garages carry it.

Energy Saving Trust (www.est.org.uk)
LPG Association (www.boostlpg.co.uk)

71. If a car is essential for work, share it with others. If you only use a car occasionally, join a car club.

Are you going solo? Up to 80 per cent of cars travelling to work in rush hours have only one driver.

If public transport to work is difficult, and cycling there too far, you could think of moving nearer or working at home some days. But when a car is essential, find out if anyone at work lives somewhere near you and share it.

The average car commuter drives 19 miles a day. Cutting that by half through car sharing would save 648 kg of carbon dioxide a year. That's no mean contribution.

You can also share your car for shopping, taking children to school, going to a sports fixture, getting to or from university, etc. A number of websites can help you find people to share with.

78

If you only occasionally need a vehicle, consider joining a car club. With this type of club, users have a pool of cars to drive. They book in advance through a central office, anything from a day to an hour, pick up at a designated parking bay and access the vehicle with a smart card. They pay a monthly fee and are billed for hours hired and miles driven. There are now car clubs in 29 UK towns and cities and 2,500 users.

For people to share your car with, go to:
www.liftshare.org
www.nationalcarshare.co.uk
www.shareacar.com

For car clubs, go to:
www.carclubs.org.uk

72. Slow down – driving at high speeds uses more fuel and causes more emissions.

Driving at high speed uses more fuel and causes more pollution. Fuel consumption and pollution increase above 50 mph, and particularly above 60 mph.

Emissions are estimated to be 19 per cent higher if a car is driven at 60 mph than 50 mph; and 48 per cent higher if driven at 70 mph rather than 50 mph.

Driving slower is also safer. You have more time to react. And imagine the unthinkable – that you hit a wall. Would you prefer to hit it at 30 mph or 70 mph?

Other aspects of motoring that can contribute to increased fuel consumption and emissions are incorrect tyre pressure, aggressive driving style, a ski-box on the roof, leaving the rear screen heater (demister) switched on, air conditioning and the sun roof open.

See North Lanarkshire Council
(www.northlan.gov.uk)
Click on SMARTways/What Drivers Should Know!/Your Speed

73. Shop at local shops. Campaign against hypermarket expansion in the high street.

If you shop by car, cut down the miles you travel and pollutants emitted by shopping as near to home as you can. Locally owned shops make for cultural diversity and may stock more local produce.

But local shops are under threat, In 2004, a record 2,157 small-scale shops closed down in the UK, according to the Institute of Grocery Distribution – that's about 8 per cent of all our small-scale shops. It compares with 300 closures in 2003. If this trend continues, small shops in Britain could be almost wiped out within 12 years.

The US-based Institute for Local Self-Reliance has had success in some areas of the US in halting big shop expansion (www.ilsr.org).

In the UK, the New Economics Foundation has raised awareness of the issues, with a report 'Clone Town Britain' (www.neweconomics.org).

Consider also becoming involved in a Local Economic Trading System (www.gmlets.u-net.com). Also, www.nottingham.ac.uk.

And shop at farmers' markets and subscribe to local box schemes where possible. See www.localfoodworks.org.

74. Calculate how far your food has travelled.

Examine your meal carefully – the lamb might be from New Zealand, the peas from Zimbabwe, the garlic from Chile, the apples from South Africa . . . the list is endless.

Do a rough calculation as to how far the food in front of you has travelled to be there. Much of it will have come by air. Some goods, like coffee and tea, cannot be grown in the UK, but much of our food could be grown more locally. Work out how much of what you eat could have been produced within miles of you rather than thousands of miles.

'The real cost of food miles madness are seldom reflected in the price of food,' says Hugh Raven of SAFE Alliance. Those costs do not just include emissions from air transport. They also come from 'diverting land in food-deficit countries from producing food for local consumption into crops'.*

The further that food has travelled the less sustainable and the less environmentally friendly it is. So think 'miles travelled' when you shop.

* The Food Miles Report, SAFE Alliance
(www.sustainweb.org).

75. Buy online instead of driving to the shops.

Most food shops now have an online service. Instead of driving to the shop, order your food online and let the shop bring it to you.

The delivery vehicle will, of course, be using fuel but it may be delivering to several homes nearby at the same time. So there should be an overall saving in fuel used.

The range of goods you can buy online is, of course, much wider than food and drink. There are a vast number of online sellers of different merchandise.

So if you want to cut down on your use of fuel, and if cycling or using public transport is not an option, seriously consider switching to online shopping.

76. Press your local authority for more cycle lanes and public transport.

Most towns and cities now have cycle lanes. If there are none, or very few in your town, start a campaign for more. Your local authority is likely to be well aware of mounting traffic problems and is looking for ways to solve them.

Remind officials and councillors that cycle lanes can be provided at low cost. And that the economic benefits of getting cars off the road are considerable – quicker journey times to work, quicker times for delivery vehicles, etc.

Consider campaigning also for improved public transport and bus lanes. When buses have their own lanes, they can deliver people to work faster than private cars.

A third of the public say they would travel less by car if local bus services were better, found a Commission for Integrated Transport report in 2002. Improved punctuality and reliability and improved frequency were the priorities for improvement among those who would travel less by car (www.cfit.gov.uk/reports/mori2002/05.htm).

The CTC campaigns for improved cycling facilities: CTC, Cotterel House, 69 Meadrow, Godalming, GU7 3HS, tel: 0870 873 0069 (www.ctc.org.uk).

77. Recycle all you can.

Redemption – we all stand in need of it. But let's include our goods as well as ourselves. Let's redeem – recycle – as much as possible. In Britain we recycle 17 per cent of what we use. That's less than any other country in Western Europe.

Make full use of local recycling facilities. Local councils are obliged to reduce the amount of waste going into landfill sites. Most councils now collect papers, plastics and cans separately from other household waste. Press your council to do more. Go beyond this level, however, and recycle your old mobile phone, printer, fax and printer cartridges. Doing this can help small-scale producers in the developing world.

Traidcraft has teamed up with a leading recycling company called Eurosource. Every time you donate a cartridge or old mobile phone to Eurosource, Traidcraft receives a donation. An estimated 105 million mobile phones are replaced in Europe each year. Many are in good working order. They can be useful in developing countries which do not have a comprehensive landline infrastructure.

Freepost bags in which to post your cartridges and phones are available from Eurosource (tel. 08451 302010). When you ring, mention that you would like to support Traidcraft by sending in used cartridges or phones. If you have a large number of cartridges, or would like to encourage your employer or a local group to become involved in larger collections, Eurosource can provide free collections.

Go further still and recycle old computers. They could be welcome in another community. Computer Aid International recycles computers from Britain for use in schools and community organizations in developing countries (433 Holloway Road, London N7 6LJ, tel: 020 7281 0091, www. computer-aid.org).

Go to www.freecycle.org to offer your unwanted goods free to others.

78. Switch off!

This is just about the only one of the 100 ways in this book when the advice is – switch off!

But switch off your electrical devices – completely – when you've finished using them. Don't leave them on standby. Computers, televisions and videos left on standby can use around 60 per cent as much electricity as when they are fully on.

And take a look at the wonderfully named TV-B-Gone. This is a keychain that turns off virtually any television set. When it came out in the United States in December 2004 it was in such demand that the TV-B-Gone website crashed. By the second day, they had sold out.

The device, which looks like a vehicle remote key, has a single button. When activated, it flashes out over 200 different codes to turn off televisions.

Volunteers in the US and America and Britain took part in 2005 in protests against televisions in public places. This is co-ordinated by White Dot, an international campaign against television (www.whitedot.org/issue/iss_front.asp).

And will the last person to leave a room in your house . . . please switch off the light.

A TV-B-Gone device costs $14.99 (www.tvbgone.com).

79. Buy devices for your home which are energy efficient – low-energy light bulbs, kitchen machinery, loft insulation, double-glazing, etc.

New technologies make it possible for us to reduce by a sizeable amount the energy we need in our home. Washing machines, dishwashers, spin driers, cookers, fridges, freezers, televisions, videos are all more energy-efficient than they were – but there are variations.

When you buy a washing machine, etc. look carefully at the labels and buy one as energy-efficient as possible. If possible buy devices with a A, AA or AAA rating.

Fit energy-saving compact fluorescent light bulbs. Compact fluorescent, halogen and sodium lighting come in many forms and designs. Ask a local dealer for suggestions.

Cut down heat loss from your home by fitting loft insulation and double or triple-glazing.

Being green in your choice of appliances will help reduce carbon dioxide emissions, and save you money.

For advice, call your nearest Energy Efficiency Advice Centre free on 0800 512012 (www.natenergy.org.uk/ensave1.htm).

80. Turn down your central heating if it doesn't harm your health. Warm yourself rather than the air around you.

If you turn down the central heating thermostat in your home by one degree, you will hardly notice the difference. You will save money and the planet will gain. And turn off the heating when you leave the house.

Be more ambitious and decide to wear warmer clothes around the house in winter, and to turn down the thermostat by several degrees. Work on the principle that you, the planet and the poor will gain if you warm yourself rather than the air around you. (If you're very elderly, make really sure that you do keep warm. It does not help anyone if you harm your health.)

If you visit a public building and the heat is fierce and the windows wide open – complain!

For other ways of saving energy in the home, see: www.natenergy.org.uk/ensave1.htm.

81. If you see lights blazing away at night in offices or work units near you, write to the company.

It is an all too common sight! – lights blazing away in offices at night, even computers left switched on. What a waste of resources. It doesn't concern you, it's just a matter for them? No, it's a matter for us all.

But don't just grumble, do something. Write to the company and say that you have a sure-fire way of saving them money – and for stepping up their social responsibility rating. Ask for a meeting, remind them of electricity's contribution to global warming.

If you get nowhere, take pictures, tell your local press. If the practice continues, and it's a public company, buy a single share and go to their annual meeting to raise the issue. And keep on doing so until darkness descends over their office block at night.

82. Don't let the sun and the wind go to waste. Install solar panels or small wind turbines on your roof to obtain some of your electricity from these renewable sources.

The sun beats down and bakes our houses in summer, the winds blow and knock tiles off the roof in winter storms. We know the power of sun and wind, let's use it. Solar and wind power have the huge advantage that they do not create carbon dioxide. Harnessing these natural, clean, renewable forms of energy is essential.

Solar power is increasingly being used for heating water, producing electricity and for heating and lighting. Panels are attached on the roof of a house which contain pipes. When the sun hits the panels and the pipes, power is generated. If, at times, the electricity produced is more than is needed in the home, the surplus can be fed into the national electricity grid.

The saving with a solar systems depends on how much sun falls on your roof, which depends on which direction your house faces – south and south-west are good. A solar system may take a number of years to pay you back – but it starts paying the environment back immediately.

For harnessing wind power, you can fit a generator about the size of a shoe box on the roof or on a wall so that it catches the prevailing wind. This could provide around 15 per cent of a household's electricity needs.

And for clothes drying . . . the sun and the wind mean that the best clothes drier on the market is an outside washing line.

For more information on solar and wind energy go to the greenenergy website of the National Energy Foundation (www.nef.org.uk/greenenergy).

For wind power, see also the Windsave website (www.windsave.com).

83. Take a shower rather than a bath – you could use less than half the electricity.

By taking a shower you can use much less hot water and hence electricity than taking a bath, maybe a third to a half as much. Don't install a power shower, however. These can use up to twice as much water as a bath!

Be aware that the older the showerhead, the more water it uses. Newer showerheads deliver 2.5 gallons per minute, while older ones deliver up to 8 gallons per minute, according to Southwest Florida Water Management District.

A shower has the advantage over a bath that a constant temperature is maintained. Also that the water is constantly clean.

Try installing an ultra low-flow showerhead. And the shorter you shower the more energy you will save.

And if it has to be a bath – before starting the water flow, plug your tub and turn the water on only slightly while adjusting to the desired temperature. Bathe small children together. And, as for yourself, share your bath if you can with someone you know extremely well!

84. Decline plastic carrier bags in shops and supermarkets. In France, many supermarkets no longer hand them out.

Our planet is being choked. The culprit? Plastic bags. Billions of them, literally billions are given out each year – 8 billion a year in Britain alone, the equivalent of 135 per person. (Why should anyone need 135 plastic carrier bags?!) Like free trade, these 'free' bags cost us dearly.

Plastic bags start as 'crude oil, natural gas, or other petrochemical derivatives. These are transformed into chains of hydrogen and carbon molecules known as polymers or polymer resin. After being heated, shaped, and cooled, the plastic is ready to be flattened, sealed, punched, or printed on.'* The key point is that their production demands vast amounts of oil.

They start as oil, and end as ugly litter. Eventually the bags break down into tiny toxic bits, polluting soils, rivers, lakes and oceans.

So refuse to accept plastic bags. Take your own durable shopping bag to the shops. In 2005 a number of French supermarkets stopped handing out plastic bags. Campaign for Britain to follow.

*www.worldwatch.org/pubs/goodstuff/plasticbags

85. Don't shop on at least one day a week. Reclaim Sunday as a no-shopping day.

Britain has become 'a nation of obsessed shoppers,' says the Bishop of Manchester, the Rt Revd Nigel McCulloch. 'The temple-like structures of some supermarkets and shopping malls suggest shopping is a new religion,' he writes in *Manchester News* (December 2004, www.manchesteronline.co.uk); 'but it has a heavy price, bringing extra strain on families, closure of local shops, and unwelcome increases in traffic and pollution.'

'God knew what he was doing when he ordained a day of rest. But, sadly, the disease of activism has infected us all. No wonder most people have little time for God when even Christians ignore the psalmist's compelling reminder that to know God we need to be still,' writes the bishop.

Shops may be open on Sunday, but that doesn't mean you have to use them. So take a stand. Buy a newspaper from a local shop if that's your tradition, but shun shopping centres. If enough people do so, it will have an impact.

To support the ongoing Keep Sunday Special campaign, contact John Alexander, Campaign Manager, 3 Hooper Street,

Cambridge CB1 2NZ, tel: 01223 566319 (www.jubilee-centre. org/kss).

86. Eat differently.

When animals are reared for beef in feedlots it can take 7 lbs of grain to produce 1 lb of meat. With pork and chicken the ration is lower, but still around 3 lbs to 1 lb.

This type of meat production is, therefore, grossly inefficient in terms of resource use. And it can have severe knock-on effects. It can force up the world price of grain and cause developing countries that are often importers of grain – about two-thirds of them – to have to dig deeper into their often limited foreign exchange kitties to buy food when domestic supplies are not enough. Or they have to cut back, to the detriment of the poor.

Beef-cattle, pigs and chickens can, however, be fed on grass. So watch for the labels. If you buy meat and poultry, buy grass-fed if you can. Or take the more radical option and give up meat altogether.

87. Cook for friends and neighbours.

As you cook your evening meal, say for two people, a couple next door may be doing the same, and the household next door to them. If you come together for a meal on a regular basis, there will be a reduction in the gas or electricity used and friendships will blossom into the bargain.

Large quantities of food take less energy to cook than the same quantity in individual portions. They also require less packaging than small amounts added together. So again there is an energy saving.

But don't just think friends and neighbours. Encourage people in your church or football club, for example, to cook and eat together on a regular basis.

Cooking for friends has the added benefit that it's a mark of respect for and celebration of that friendship. Eating together is a shared experience that can help to break down barriers and deepen understanding.

Save a little more energy by eating together by candlelight . . . who knows what that might start!

88. Share electrical devices with your friends and neighbours. Wash your clothes with them instead of doing half-empty loads.

That hedge trimmer you use once a year. Funny, your neighbour has a very similar one. That electrical saw who use a few times over the winter to cut up your logs. Again your neighbour has much the same thing. You can extend the list further . . .

Household electrical devices take a lot of energy to manufacture and are often underused. So talk with neighbours, family and friends and discuss which appliances you could buy together and jointly own. It might even extend to the lawn-mower.

Think too of your washing machine. If it's often the case that you run it on half-empty loads, again talk with neighbours, etc. and consider washing your clothes together. It all helps.

89. Wash dishes by hand. If you use a dishwasher, only start it when it's full.

There's a great website called e-how – 'Clear Instructions on How To Do (just about) Everything' (www.ehow.com). It's well worth a visit for all sorts of reasons.

One of the issues on the site is 'How to Clean and Dry Dishes by Hand'. Well, as it says, with automatic dishwashers doing all the work for us, 'you may have forgotten how to do the simple task of washing dishes by hand'. So it gives a quick review – which turns out to have some very useful reminders.

As hot water is normally used for washing dishes, there is an energy cost, no matter which method you use. If you use a very energy-efficient dishwater, and only start it when it's packed full, you may not be using more energy than washing dishes by hand. Circumstances will of course vary. But if you start your dishwasher when it's only half-full, you've hardly a teaspoon to stand on.

90. Put the kettle on – don't fill it!

All over Britain, kettle madness has taken hold. Kettles are being filled – literally filled. Water is being boiled that isn't needed, a cup of water is poured onto tea, coffee, chocolate, whatever – and the rest of the boiled water is thrown away.

If you're part of this madness, it's costing you money and the environment dear. The good news is that you can end it the very next time you pour water into your kettle.

Terminology is important here. Instead of saying let's 'fill the kettle', let's talk rather of 'putting the kettle on', or 'cupping' the kettle, 'two-cupping' it, whatever. Pour into the kettle enough water for the cups you need. Remember, however, to cover the heating element.

This means you need to take care when you buy a new kettle. Some require that you fill them with a minimum of half a litre of water, for example. But maybe you don't want that much. Perhaps you only need to boil enough for one or two cups at a time. It's worth looking at travel kettles,. So buy a kettle that meets your needs – and the environment's.

Six

Rising to challenges

91. Pray as if making poverty history depends on it.

Prayer is the most important action a Christian can take. It was only by prayer, for example, that Jesus said it was possible to heal when a boy with an evil spirit was brought to him (Mark 9:14–29).

Faithful, purposeful, regular, committed prayer is a vital Christian contribution to making poverty history. 'More things are wrought by prayer than this world dreams of' wrote Tennyson.

Jesus taught us to pray 'give us this day our daily bread'. When you pray these words, pray for *all of us*, every child, woman and man, to have enough bread, rice, cassava, sorghum, potato, whatever is a person's staple food. So when you pray the Lord's Prayer you are praying for policies that will ensure enough bread on the tables of the 800 million people who do not have enough – and you are committing yourself to action to see that happen.

With God, all things are possible. Prayer leads us to action. An ancient Hebrew prayer runs: 'Pray as if everything depended on God. Act as if everything depended on you.'

'Expect great things of God . . . attempt great things for God,' wrote William Carey, who is known as the 'Father of Modern Missions'.

Making poverty history is a modern mission. Working for this mission, seeing it through until it is thoroughly accomplished, is a great thing for God. Pray for it, attempt it, expect it.

92. Tithe. Give away 10 per cent of your net take-home pay – a good slice of it to anti-poverty projects.

Tithing – giving one tenth of your income – dates back to some of the earliest figures in the Bible. 'Then Abram gave him [Melchizedek, king of Salem] a tenth of everything' (Genesis 14:20b). This was confirmed by Jacob in Genesis 28:20–22, but this time the vow was to God: 'of all that you give me I will give a tenth'.

Tithing became the norm of Jewish tradition. But Jesus made it clear that tithing is not enough in itself: 'Woe to you Pharisees because you give God a tenth . . . but you neglect justice and the love of God' (Luke 11:42a).

There is a strong case for Christians to tithe today, not for legalistic reasons, but out of love. At least some of the money that results could help to fund projects that further the cause of justice for the poor.

Some believe that today's taxation system distributes money from rich to poor and can be seen as a modern-day system of tithing. But when we look at the poverty that exists, giving a tenth of net take-home pay might still be considered not only necessary, but vital.

So let tithing be a symbol of your willingness to share with the poor.

93. Be a prophet! Warn of what could happen if nothing happens.

If nothing happens, if poverty is not made history, the future is bleak. It's already bleak for around a quarter of humanity. But poverty will not stand still, it will either be defeated or increase.

If nothing happens, even more babies will be stunted and die. Bewildered and hungry people will scamper into boats to seek life, any life, in western countries. Who can blame them when the gap between them and the West has grown so large.

We are a part of the suffering of others: 'Any man's death diminishes me,' wrote John Donne, 'because I am involved in mankind.' But there is self-interest too for we cannot expect to survive as a rich island in a sea of poverty.

Christians have a prophetic role to play. Taking the trouble to be informed about what is going on lays the basis for informing and warning others what is happening.

Don't expect to be thanked for it. The Old Testament prophets were often reviled, often seen as uncomfortable people to have around. When, for example, Ezekiel warned 'their silver and gold will not be able to save them in the days of the Lord's wrath' (7:19), he could have hardly have been the most popular guy in town. Such considerations did not stop the prophets saying what they believed to be right.

94. Be ready with answers when people tell you that you've got it all wrong.

You might be told that poverty is nothing to do with trade, aid and debt relief, that people are poor because they have too many kids. Where there is poverty, people tend to have large families. Not all will survive, and those who do survive will help their parents in old age. Most countries cannot afford pensions. Children are seen as insurance. The way to reduce population growth is to beat poverty.

Again, you will be told that it's because of corruption that people are poor. Corruption is a factor. And it exists at different levels. At the international level it's practised largely by transnational corporations, often involving large sums of money. Corruption needs rooting out at international, national and local levels. Where there is poverty, corruption is again more likely to be found. Tackling poverty is also tackling corruption.

99

'Make poverty history?' I've been asked, 'Jesus said the poor you will always have with you' (Matthew 26:11). These words come in the story of the woman who poured expensive perfume on Jesus. But he was responding to the self-righteous misreading of the woman's devotion. And Jesus was reminding the disciples that the only reason there are poor in the abundant world that God created is because of human sin and self-centredness – because we fail to love as we should.

There are many examples of the concern of Jesus and the early Christians for the poor, such as 'I was hungry and you gave me something to eat' (Matthew 25:35) and 'there were no needy persons among them' (Acts 4:34a).

If someone raises an issue and you don't know the answer, say so, but find it (ask Christian Aid, for example) and get back to them soon.

95. Show solidarity with the poor by fasting regularly.

When Jesus talked about fasting he did not say 'if' but 'when': 'When you fast . . .' (Matthew 6:16). Fasting, together with prayer and penitence, has been practised since early Old Testament days. Jesus accepted fasting as a natural discipline.

Fasting is also seen as preparation for new ventures. Paul describes fasting before his baptism, for example (Acts 9:9). Some Christians in New Zealand were planning in late May 2005 to fast for 40 days before the G8 summit in July.

Muslims go without food from dawn to dusk each year in the 30-day period of Ramadan. If you're reasonably healthy, why not try it next Lent?

Fasting should never be for show, it must always be accompanied by a concern for social justice, warns the prophet Isaiah (chapter 58).

Fasting could make you tired, you may not be able to work as much, but take care that it does not make you irritable.

It must not deflect you from being your best! Wesley recommended fasting two days a week until 3 p.m.

In a very tiny way, your voluntary fasting shows solidarity with those who involuntarily have to go without food.

96. Question your concept of prosperity. Look at the Buddhist concept of prosperity.

Do you measure your prosperity in terms of how much money you have? It's useful to look at Buddhism.

From the Buddhist perspective a prosperous person is self-reliant, has self-dignity and is proud of his or her culture, is humble and values simplicity (in short has contentment), is generous, and is ever mindful.

You don't have to be Buddhist to hold much in common with that position. Christians would emphasize perhaps that they are dependent on God and not on themselves, they may want to add a caveat about pride, but would agree with humility, generosity and being ever mindful.

But there's something interesting that is missing from the Buddhist concept of prosperity – there is no mention of wealth or income. How much money a person has is not seen as important to how prosperous a person is.

We could all learn a great deal from that. Jesus warned that we cannot serve God and money. He spoke of the dangers of money, that it's easier for a camel to go through the eye of a needle than for a rich man to enter the kingdom of heaven. And Paul warned that the love of money is the root of all evil.

97. Set yourself a target. Ask – 'How many of the things in this book am I doing?' Within three months, six months, a year, how many could you be doing?

Some of the things in this book you are likely be doing already. You may doing a sizeable number. But whatever level you are at, set yourself a target – decide how many you could be doing within six weeks, three months, six months, a year.

Better to have a target that you fall short of than no target at all. Monitor your target regularly.

Make sure you aim to do a number of ways from every section as they reinforce and complement each other.

Be ambitious but don't be discouraged if you fall short of your target.

Likewise, don't be too easily satisfied with your efforts. Don't just stop filling your kettle to the brim with water, for example, and sit back and feel you've done enough!

98. Expect success. If you expect failure or defeat you'll be defensive, and that's more likely to generate opposition than if you demonstrate that you expect success.

Towards the end of May 2005, ministers of European Union countries agreed to double the aid their countries give to the world's poor. This came soon after an announcement by the British government that it would no longer impose economic polices on developing countries as the price for aid.

The government has also started to change its position on trade, even including a pledge in its election manifesto to stop bullying developing countries.

Policy announcements feed no one. Now we need to insist that policies are translated into action.

But why the change in government policy? Could it have something to do with the fact that the Make Poverty History campaigners were so positive and so insistent that government could not ignore them? That ministers acted because they had to act, because people were expecting them to act?

So work for success and expect success. Go on the offensive. Your enthusiasm, your commitment makes a difference. There will be setbacks. Continuous progress is unlikely. When setbacks happen, pick yourself up and start again.

99. Buy another copy of this book and give it to a friend.

This is the shortest entry in the book. I would not wish to delay you for a moment in going out and buying another copy to give to a friend.

Please tell your friend that this is a 'must read now book' because the task of making poverty history will be strengthened by their presence. And they too might want to buy a copy for a friend . . .

100. Give birth to your own new and innovative ways of making poverty history. (The ideas in these pages are by no means exhaustive.)

While researching this book I came across a title *500 Ways to Annoy Your Roommate*. It reminded me of the sheer depth of human ingenuity! That someone could come up with so many ways to annoy a roommate. (I'd have thought your roommate would have walked out long before you reached 500.)

And if there can be 500 ways to annoy a roommate, then how many ways can there to make poverty history? This book has 100. These are by no means exhaustive, but I happen to believe they cover the main ways – that's why they're in the book! But you may know better. You may already be putting into practice other ways of making poverty history. And you may be determined that you will find yet more ways.

So use a sheet of paper in the back of this book. Add new ways as you go along. And share them with others. You can post them on the website that accompanies this book: www. canterburypress/100waystomakepovertyhistory

You *can* change the world!